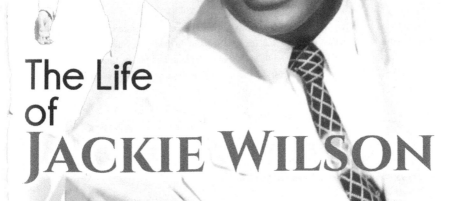

The Life
of
JACKIE WILSON

The Legacy
Continues

Brenda Wilson

Front Cover Design by Andrea Butler, illmaginable Designs
Illmaginabledesigns.wixsite.com/illdesigns,
586-422-7940, illmaginabledesigns@gmail.com

Edited by Dr. Mary Edwards
Leaves of Gold Consulting, LLC—LeavesOfGoldConsulting.com
Editor does a disclaimer on the accuracy of all scripture.

Book Design by Shannon Crowley
Treasure Image & Publishing—TreasureImagePublishing.com

DEDICATION

This book was inspired by my mother, Susie Gipson, and my father the late great Jackie Wilson. This a Love Project from my heart, in loving memory to both my parents. Mama and Daddy, I will never forget you and I will always remember the love that radiated from your hearts.

A very, very, special thank you to all the wonderful people who gave me their support and dedication while producing this book … I am truly grateful.

While finalizing this book our brother, Thor Kenneth Wilson, made his transition on October 23, 2018. "We Love You Thor." RIP. You will truly be missed by many.

LOVE ALWAYS!
Brenda

CONTENTS

ACKNOWLEDGEMENTS

As I traveled down memory lane, so many faces, names and places came to my mind. Please forgive me if I didn't mention you. Count it to my head and not my heart.

First, I would like to acknowledge the Jackie Wilson family for their support and kindness, and especially my children: Roscoe III, Alicia, Angelica, Lizzie and Erika who are all very loving, talented, educated with degrees, accomplished, dedicated men and women of God with integrity. They have supported and stuck by me down through the years no matter what idea I came up with and decided I wanted to do. They were there right beside me.

Thanks to Opal Hodge who I truly call my friend, my spiritual sister, who has always been with me since 1990. Without her assistance on every show we have done, I don't think I could have been successful. She would always tell me what the word of God said for every situation we were going through. I love you!

Special thanks to Dr. LaToya Patman for her support, guidance, and her willingness to be a blessing in all areas of my life and the life of my family. Thank you. Much love and blessings to you.

Special thanks to Dr. Delores Brown for her support and the love that she shared with the Jackie Wilson family, as well as the story she told. Love and blessings always.

Special thanks to Ann Caver for her love and support, and to my nieces and nephews Theresa Retonia, Latricia, Felicia and Robert Caver down through the years.

Special thanks to Lamont and Cheryl Robinson for all their help and support down through the years for the Jackie Wilson Foundation.

Special thanks to David Washington, TV One Unsung Heroes, who's always been there to help and support when I call. Thank you and God bless you always.

A special, special, thanks to Uncle Billy Davis who's always been there to support and help in any way that he could. He was my daddy's best friend.

I thank him for all his knowledge and his memories that he shared for this book. Love you, Uncle Billy Davis.

Special thanks to Ronald Lockett, executive director, and Gail Carr, director over sales and events, at the Northwest Activities center for all your support and help to make our events a big success. Thank you and we love you both.

Special thanks to my great security team M.I.P.R.S. These men and women are wonderful. I am very thankful and grateful for their service. Love you

Special acknowledgements for all your help and support to Lena Towers, Melvin Davis, Entertainment Ambassador, Lamont and Cheryl Robinson for contributing your memories and photos.

Special thanks to Bert Dearing of Bert's Warehouse Theatre in Detroit for all his generosity and support that he has always given to me and the Jackie Wilson Foundation and the love he has shown posthumously for Jackie Wilson. We love you Bert and the community thank you for all your support as well.

Special thanks to all our teams of volunteers throughout the 30 years of doing music showcases, VIP receptions, parties, prom send offs, TV shows, interviews, and any other creative ideas I had. I could always call and depend on: Master Sergeant Roscoe Johnson II, Alicia Miller, Angelica Johnson, Lizzie Johnson-Petty, Erika Johnson, Pat Ford, Cheryl Ford, Crystal Ridgeway, Felicia Walker-Hayes, Brian James, Ashley Thompson, Lady Champagne, Gisele Caver. Special thanks to Jerry Brooks and the Band: Steve Jackson, keyboard, Bill Malone, keyboard, James Francis, bass, and Baby Ray drummer. They always do a great job. Thank you very much.

Special thanks to Dr. Roman Franklin, "Dr. Doo Wop." I thank him for his never-ending support for Jackie and Brenda Wilson. Dr. Doo Wop is a lover of music, a standup comedian and a historian of music. He has traveled far and wide as a record collector and also has been a sponsor for our shows and hosted many events.

Most recently, he was a vital part of the team that went to Hollywood for the placement of the Jackie Wilson Star on the Hollywood Walk of Fame.

Special Thanks to 3K Sports, Vev Tripp—State Farm agency, Impact Detroit Magazine, Tim Horton in Highland Park, Lizzie Johnson, Erika Johnson and Roscoe Johnson for the support.

Thanks to all my Master of Ceremonies, John Mason, Tune-Up Man, Gerald McBride, Lamont Robinson and Greg Dunmore for their support down through the years. Thanks to all my Social Media Supporters.

Thanks to my buddy, Elijah Jacobs for his kindness, support and love.

Thank you everyone for your prayers and I hope you enjoy the book.

FOREWORD

Mr. Excitement: Jackie Wilson

Mary Wilson, The Supremes

Growing up in Detroit, Michigan, in the 1960s, was magical. It was the early days of rock and roll, and doo-wop was what every vocal group was singing. Also, black male idols were emerging.

At a very young age, I recall hearing my Uncle John L's music collection, which included the likes of Joe Williams, Louis Armstrong and, of course, the mid-'60s brought "Mr. Excitement," Jackie Wilson.

In Negro communities, music was everywhere: jazz, gospel and rock and roll. It didn't matter what genre. Music was the number one entertainment in every household.

When I first heard Mr. Excitement, aka Jackie Wilson, on the radio, I was in love. I was barely a teenager, but I fell in love with his voice. At the time, I had no idea that he grew up just a few neighborhoods from where I was living in the Brewster-Douglass projects. However, I was soon to realize that there were many other up and coming artists living in the same close neighborhoods.

Jackie Wilson's style was young and full of energy. He brought class, style and youth to his music. He had the sexiest smile and just a hint of naughty, but in a boyish way. It was clean, with just a hint of sultriness that had the women swooning over him. Also, he had the wisp of a curl falling from the then popular hairstyle of the marcel look the colored guys were sporting then. I bet Elvis stole it from Jackie.

His dancing was as great as his singing. He would do a few turns in the middle of a phrase, then before you could bat an eye, he would fall down on his knees into a full split, sometimes two of them. The moonwalk was maybe not invented by him, but he was doing it before James Brown or Michael Jackson.

Coming in a rock and roll genre, he was classy.

Mr. Excitement was also a great singer with a full two or three octaves. He could have been a cantor or opera singer with that voice.

There were not a lot of TV shows to see our favorite black acts back then, but all of the local radio stations played Jackie Wilson's songs. They were "Reet Petite," "Doggin' Around," "Baby Workout," "Lonely Teardrops" and "Higher and Higher." All of his earlier singing in the Billups Chapel and with Billy Ward and his Dominoes came into play in his recordings.

I finally got the chance to see Mr. Jackie Wilson when I was old enough to get into the Graystone Ballroom. It was one of my first concerts. We had started singing as the Primettes in 1959 and were doing local DJ shows in Detroit on the weekends. Seeing Jackie Wilson, a real pro, opened my eyes at the age of 14 to show business and, perhaps without my even realizing it, hooked me into being an entertainer.

Years later, the Supremes were on a chitterling circuit gig at the Royal Theatre in Baltimore, Maryland, with other acts, including Jackie Wilson. It was a real rush for us.

Diane's mom asked Jackie Wilson to babysit us while she ran out to get something to eat between shows. He said yes and we all just nearly died. Wow, Mr. Wilson was a real gentleman and told us with a wink to be good.

Yes, Mr. Jackie Wilson had the magic touch.

INTRODUCTION

In this publication, I am sharing with the readers the stories about my father that I hold very dear in my heart. These are my personal experiences and stories that have been shared with me by my mother, family members, and fans.

I am very proud of my father, Jackie Wilson, who was one of the greatest entertainers in the world. My father had a lot of love to give and was loved by many all over the world. During his lifetime, he had many relationships and many friends, some good and some not so good. And he had a significant impact on a lot of people's lives all over the world with his operatic, four-octave voice. He sang his songs with excitement and love. His performances displayed a handsome man with charisma and charm. "They say you either have it or you don't."

Jackie Wilson, known as "Mr. Excitement," had the "It Factor." This was the compelling attractiveness and force of personality combined with a personal magic that aroused his family, friends and fans to the brink of hysteria. It made the crowds uncontrollable—in a good way!

I am sure that many of you knew and loved him as Jackie Wilson, Jack or even Sonny and that you have many wonderful stories to tell from your experiences. I wish that I could have met you to share your exciting memories of him.

Like my father, I love to sing and I am carrying on his legacy. But God has given me a greater gift, and it is the ability to love others. I can truly say that I love being a blessing to others. That is why I have done so many things to keep his memories alive through the establishment of the Jackie Wilson Foundation, Inc., www.jackiewilson foundation.org.

God is love and love comes easy for me because it's a characteristic of my Heavenly Father and my earthly father, Jackie Wilson. Jackie showed love to everyone he met—and extended his love when he kissed the girls and said goodbye.

CHAPTER ONE

A Superstar is Born

When you hear the name, "Jackie Wilson," so many wonderful memories come to mind. In this book, I will paint a picture of the great man during his lifetime. Jackie was a lot more than a great singer. He was a complete entertainer. Mr. Excitement, a great father, great uncle, great brother, and a great friend. In fact, I consider him to be one of the greatest entertainers who ever lived. He was a songwriter and "a singer's singer"— or better yet a sanger's sanger, meaning he sang straight from his soul.

Jackie's style, a fusion of 1950s doo-wop, rock and blues in soul music, was a sound people hadn't heard before. He was new and refreshing, which created "Mr. Excitement."

Jackie reached his audience with words as well as his style. He touched the very core of human emotions and pulled on the heartstrings of the world with his lyrics. He made people smile and brought enjoyment and excitement to all who came in contact with him.

Jack (Sonny) Leroy "Jackie" Wilson Jr., "Mr. Excitement," was born on Saturday, June 9, 1934, at Herman Kiefer Hospital in Detroit. (I, Brenda Wilson, was born in the same hospital.) From there, newborn Jackie was taken home to Highland Park, Michigan.

He was the only son of singer and songwriter Jack Leroy Wilson, Sr. (1897-1949), and Eliza Mae Wilson, Née Ransom (1907-1984), who was a singer in her own right. From 1935 to 1940, they lived at 7958 Russell St., until Jack Jr. was five years old. His mother was originally from Columbus, Mississippi, and his father, my grandfather, was from Kennedy, Alabama. Jack Jr., known as Sonny, was the only surviving child of this marriage, which made him very special to his mother, who adored and loved the ground he walked on.

To his family and friends, he was known as "Sonny," and that nickname followed him his entire life.

The family later moved to 1533 Lyman Place in Detroit, a community just a stone's throw from Highland Park, Michigan. Lyman Street was a part of the Metro Detroit area called the North End, and this was where Jackie would spend a lot of his time as a child. Highland Park was an area of about three—square miles surrounded by the city of Detroit and was thought to be a tough Detroit-area neighborhood. Some years later, the family moved to 248 Cottage Grove St., near Woodward Avenue, also in Highland Park.

His mother took him to church, and with her background in music, she was his first musical inspiration. He was raised and baptized in the Russell Street Missionary Baptist Church. His mother would often say, "He had a voice that could only have come from God." He began singing from the time he was five years old. As a young boy, his voice astounded people and he would go to different places to sing, especially in local churches.

Sonny would always say with absolute certainty that he was going to become a star. He said when he made his 25¢, he was going to give his mother 15¢ and that he would keep 10¢ for himself.

Sonny also loved to read comic books. His favorite brand was Marvel Comics, and he loved the character Thor most of all. He later named one of his sons Thor.

In 1939, Jack Sr., with a fifth-grade education, worked 34 weeks as a grinder in an auto factory. Jack Sr. and Eliza Mae got a divorce in 1941. Sonny was about six years old. Later, his mother married John Lee. They had one daughter together, Joyce Lee (1945-2015). She had a divine singing voice as well. Their mother, an excellent singer herself, taught them both the ins and outs of singing in all vocal ranges.

Although, Jack (Sonny) had a happy home life with his mother; it is felt that the lack of his father's guidance in the home may have caused him to have a lot of anxiety, hurt, resentment and rebellion. These issues caused him to be incarcerated several times, beginning at the age of 12, in the Lansing Correctional Institute. When he was released, he came home and connected with some men (members in the church) and formed a gospel group called the Evereadys; of course, he was the lead singer of the group. They performed in local churches throughout Metropolitan Detroit. His only interests in high school were the glee club and the girls.

In 1947, 13-year-old Jack was a student at the respected Highland Park High School. He would go just to go, but as soon as the opportunity presented itself, he would walk right back out the door. Between the ages of 13 and 15, Sonny was consumed with his music and the young girls. -But he was not interested in school, even though school presented him with some opportunities to showcase his musical talent. Among the activities Jackie got involved with in high school was glee club.

Twins Eddie and Freddie Pride were two of Jackie's best friends. They lived in the same neighborhood and practiced singing together.

Eddie was in glee club with Jackie. His teacher was Mrs. Kent. She knew she had a star or phenomenon in Jackie and always encouraged him. She loved to hear Jackie sing, and one of the songs she loved for him to sing the most was "Silent Night."

She would ask him to sing in front of everyone. He was about 15 then. She discovered him. "You're going to make it," she always told him. "You have a golden voice." He could hit those high notes even back then. Jackie's four-octave range was uncanny.

Eventually, Eddie formed his own group called, "Eddie Pride and the Nightcaps." Eddie said, "I used to call myself a singer but after hearing Jackie, a/k/a, Sonny sing, I gave up."

As Sonny got older, his love for singing grew and was not wavering. He dedicated his time to singing more than anything else. In 1945, when he was between the ages of 10 and 12, Sonny would stand on a street corner in front of the liquor store across from White Records on Detroit's North End and sing with his childhood buddies Ralph Peterson and Freddy Pride.

He would ask people coming in and out of the store or just walking by, "Hey, do you want to hear a church song or some blues?" He would make up lyrics and sing; singing about things that were beyond his years. People thought he had so much charm and, believe it or not, that same liquor store is still in business today. His closest friends growing up included Eddie and Freddy Pride, Little Willie John, Don Hudson and Sonny's cousin Levi Stubbs (of the Four Tops). These boys looked up to Jack and, like so many other people, they were genuinely drawn to him like a magnet.

CHAPTER TWO

Freda: The Finest Girl You Ever Wanna Meet

Jackie met Freda Hood on the corner of Owens and Oakland in Highland Park, Michigan, where he was singing doo-wop and drinking wine. Jackie became friends with Don Hudson, Freda's brother, so he could get close to his sister.

Freda was so pretty and had beautiful long hair. Jackie and Freda became childhood sweethearts. He named his first song, "Reet Petite," with her in mind. He considered her to be, as the song says, "the finest girl you ever want to meet.

Although Freda was a little older than Jackie, he didn't care. Sonny loved older women.

He expressed to Freda from an early age that his ambition was to be an entertainer and he was going to marry her, too.

When Jackie was 16 and Freda 17, she became pregnant. In February 1951, they were married. A daughter was born the next month. This was the first of four children they had together: two girls and two boys.

Although Freda was Jackie's first wife, she had to deal with Jackie and his other women. She accepted the fact that he was quite a ladies' man. She knew she would have trouble on her hands. She took him unconditionally and loved his children born to other women.

Jackie had no regular job to support his new family but, from the age of 15, he had been an underage performer. The appearances brought in some cash. Still, family life was such a struggle. Because he was underage, he used someone else's ID to gain access to the club to perform — the same ID he used to get married to Freda.

Jackie was known by other names, including Elisha Richards, Sonny Wilson, Jack Leroy Wilson and Jackie Leroy Wilson. Mama Freda said he used Elisha Richards on their marriage certificate.

Early on, he expressed to Freda that his consistent ambition was to be an entertainer, which prompted him to leave school in 1949 at age 15. In addition, Sonny was singing in night clubs by this time on a regular basis. Even though he was too young to actually get into clubs like the Royal Blue Bar on Oakland Avenue in Detroit, he was still singing with the Eveready's, the group he organized at the age of 12. His performance was so amazing, he "shut it down."

At age 16, Sonny tried his hand at boxing, a new hobby that he picked up when he was in the juvenile detention center for truancy. However, his life was about singing, Freda, children, and boxing.? I guess it was my father's fate to go to juvenile detention because if it had not been for his stints there, he never would have tried boxing, where he learned his fancy footwork. His splits, his agility, and his stamina to perform for 45 minutes or more per show made him a standout showman. To this day, no one can master the boxing skips in their performance like Sonny. That's just one of the reasons why Jackie Wilson is called "Mr. Excitement."

L. Wilson

CHAPTER THREE

Opening Act: Teenager Becomes Local Celebrity

Jack, known as Sonny, started The Eveready gospel group with his good friend Ralph Peterson; a couple of other friends also were part of the group. Of course, Sonny was the lead singer. One could say Sonny began to lead a double life. He would sing in area churches, and then shoot craps at night and drink wine in the streets. Wine was his friend. He loved to entertain at the Cadillac Club, Phelps Lounge, Graystone Ballroom, Flame Showbar and many other places in Paradise Valley and Black Bottom.

Being in the streets so much exposed him to unsavory elements. So he and his cousin Levi needed to protect themselves, according to Thelma Stubbs-Mitchell, Levi's sister. They joined the well-known North End gang called the Shakers. It gave them a sense of belonging and the protection they needed. It was said that the Shakers was the toughest gang around at that time. The Shakers' territory was around Woodward Avenue, from Northern High School to five miles or so north at the junction of Eight Mile Road and Woodward, including Hamtramck.

Jackie ended up dropping out of Highland Park High School at the age of 15 because he was not focused on academics, and he was getting way too much attention from the nightlife being the entertainer. This didn't land him anywhere good. It landed him back in juvenile detention.

During his second stint in detention, he learned to box and began competing in the Detroit amateur circuit at age 16. Upon his release, Jack became a regular at Brewster Center. Rob Carter remembers when he was eight years old seeing Sonny there working out and training to become a professional boxer. His mother caught wind of him boxing and came to see him fight. When she saw the brutality of it and witnessed him taking a hit, she decided then that her son had to quit boxing. So, she forced Sonny to quit. At the time he quit boxing, he was classified as a welterweight, with a record of 8-2.

With his mother and grandmother's assistance, they redirected his focus back to singing. His love for singing increased. He put all his energy into performing and began to blossom as an entertainer. His charisma permeated through him and to the crowd like an aphrodisiac. Despite his trials and tribulations, Jackie managed to overcome many things and he became a successful entertainer.

Jackie's voice was a gift from God. No one has ever been able to successfully imitate him or sing like him. Let's be real about that. They say he had a smile that would brighten up the room. He was debonair and all of the girls took to him.

Brenda's Mother Susie

CHAPTER FOUR

Brenda's Mother, Susie: A Woman, A Lover, A Friend

Susie Mae Gibson moved from St. Petersburg, Florida to Detroit as a young girl to live with her uncle James "Bud" Gipson and her aunt Margaret. Uncle Bud had moved to the north because the job opportunities were abundant in Detroit.

He would go back to Florida each year to visit his brother William, my grandfather and grandmother Mattie Gibson and eight children. The family was always happy to see him.

One day he asked the kids who wanted to go back to Detroit and stay with him and his sister, Aunt Margaret.

Susie was the first to speak up and say, "I want to go back and live with you and Auntie."

She quickly made friends with Lillie Watson, and they went everywhere together. They attended the same schools in Hamtramck. Susie and Lillie connected because they both loved to sing.

Every life has a purpose. I guess it was predestined for her to live in Hamtramck because it was close to where Jackie lived. Susie graduated from Hamtramck High School in 1947.

Lillie and my mother would hang out at the clubs in Paradise Valley and Black Bottom. The nightlife was entertainment back in those days.

In 1948, Sonny met Susie and Lillie at a club in Paradise Valley. Mama told me that Jack, known as Sonny, was a smooth talker and that Daddy and one of his best friend, Ralph Peterson, were both fine. My dad was not called Jackie until 1953 when he started singing with Billy Ward and the Dominos.

It was easy for women to fall in love with them. I remember seeing a photo of the three of them in a club with Jackie standing between my mother and Lillie.

Sonny and Ralph would come to visit them in Hamtramck. They would walk across the tracks on Caniff Street to meet my mother and Lillie.

While Susie dated Sonny, her best friend Lillie dated Ralph. Two sets of best friends dating and having big fun. They would go to choir rehearsal in Hamtramck.

The choir director was the Rev. Frank Barnes. And then Susie got pregnant by Jackie. I am the child she was carrying in her womb. Back in those days, being pregnant and single was a "no-no," so it was kept quiet. Later, when I was old enough to ask questions, Lillie confirmed that Jackie was my father.

Rev. Barnes also confirmed that Jackie (Sonny) was my father. Rev. Barnes and Susie were members of the same congregation, Leland Baptist Church.

At that time, it was located in Hamtramck on Denton and Moran streets. Rev. Barnes said that he was the director of the Leland Baptist Choir and that Susie was one of its members.

A couple of years later, in the early 1950s, Reverend Barnes opened his own church, Temple of Prayer, and would later say, "I was both minister and choir director.

Jackie Wilson sang in the church choir along with Susie Mae, who brought their young daughter to church with her.

Susie communicated and discussed with me, her minister, a number of times that Jackie Wilson was Brenda's father." There were other confirmations along the way.

In those days, Susie had to deal with a lot of tension, being pregnant out of wedlock and having her baby girl. She later found out that Jackie had been seeing another young girl named Freda who he married two years later in 1951.

Susie's aunt and uncle were her best support system. She knew that Sonny wasn't able to take care of me and my mom.

My father, Jackie, was in my life back then at the beginning of his career. His wife, whom I always called, "Mama Freda," knew me and stated that he often brought me to my grandmother's house where everyone stayed on 248 Cottage Grove street in Highland Park, when I was a little girl. But, as Jackie started to become more and more popular, my frequent visits stopped.

My mother told me she went to see (Sonny) Jackie in the

early 1980s in the nursing home in Cherry Hill, New Jersey. When she arrived, no one was there, which was good because she could spend time alone with him.

She said that she was sickened and saddened by the state he was in and the way he looked. She told me the people at the nursing home were nice to her and that there was usually a lot of chaos with women regarding Jackie.

When she visited Jackie, he wasn't able to respond or talk to her, but she talked to him about memories from times they had together. "I am Susie, the woman who loved you," she told him. "I will always be your friend."

She asked the nursing home workers about what time other visitors usually came because she didn't want any trouble. She said that as she was asking the question in came a woman. My mother knew her as someone who was obsessed with my father and thinking she was supposed to take care of him. But she did not know who my mother was, so she whisked past her to get to Jackie.

When my mother got home and told me where she had gone, I asked her why she didn't let me go. She replied, "I didn't want you to see him like that and get caught up in any mess because if they had said anything to you, I would have had to hurt somebody."

I didn't know that the reason she went to see him was because of a tape she had seen of him in the nursing home. I said, "Ma, it's O.K." Then she showed me the tape of him in the wheelchair. I was heartbroken that someone would tape him in that state for money. I don't know who did that, but that was very cruel and demeaning. Whoever did that did not love Jackie Wilson; they loved money.

After Jackie died on January 21, 1984, Susie attended the Jan. 28th funeral. She was a nurse for her church and attended in her nursing uniform. No one even knew who she was and she served the family. My mother Susie was a loving person. She had a sense of humor and a, "Tell it like it is," personality, which was a source of great strength and joy to many. She would help anyone when she could.

Before she made her transition, she told a couple of her closest friends that she was going to be out of here on August 10th. And, just as she said, she made her transition on Aug. 10, 2007. My mother died from liver cancer. She had to be close to God to know when she was going to make her transition. Her homegoing was a celebration.

After living in Hamtramck for over 60 years, her passing affected her neighborhood and the city. The celebration emphasized the love the city had for Susie. She will truly be missed by her family and friends.

My mother loved to sing praises to God and read the Bible. She was wonderful and the best mother anyone could have. I love her and I will always miss her very, very much. Susie was truly a Woman, a Lover and a Friend to Jackie.

Celebrating The Life Of

Susie Mae Gibson

Friday, August 17, 2007

Family Hour 10:30 A.M.
Homegoing Service 11:00 A.M.

Leland Missionary Baptist Church
22420 Fenkell
Detroit, Michigan

Rev. Cecil Poe, Ph.D
Officiating Minister

Bill Ward and Dominoes with Jackie Wilson

CHAPTER FIVE

The Big Break:
Rags to Riches

Even though he was young, Jackie had a sound that could not be ignored. He was now around 16 or 17, and his golden voice with a four-octave range was getting a lot of attention.

His years of choir, glee club, singing on street corners and in nightclubs were about to pay off. He was so good that people began to pay him when he would go places to sing for them. He was a natural and had a maturity that made him seem older.

In 1953, Jackie met Sam Cooke, who was from Chicago and very charismatic and popular as well. He opened the door for Jackie, and Bristoe Bryant of WCHB gave Jackie his first opportunity on Detroit radio.

There were arenas for aspiring black singers like Jackie, amateur night at the Paradise Theater (now called Orchestra Hall), which was Detroit's equivalent of Harlem's Apollo Theater.

He also participated in the amateur nights, which also were held at Park, State, Gold Coast, Grant, and the Booker T. Warfield Theaters. These were regular movie theaters that charged 25¢ for entry and would feature 15 to 20 acts. The competition was exceptional, and the enthusiastic black audiences took the outcomes very seriously. People would come to hear and cheer for their favorite singers.

Jackie would regularly be up against the vocal talents of Little Willie John,"Singin"' Sammy Ward, Della Reese, his friends Ralph Peterson and Freddy Pride, and his cousin Levi Stubbs, who would go on to become the lead singer of the famous Four Tops.

There was another very influential singer who was often there. His name was Nolan Strong, and he achieved local success with his group the Diablos.

Jackie liked to perform "Danny Boy." He sang it in a unique way with the emotional passion that was to become his trademark. He would always win amateur nights doing "Danny Boy." When he recorded it, he did it the same way.

While he was performing in these amateur night competitions, Jackie was developing his own style of footwork, which included "falling down" splits and a crossover skip that would later become his signature move and an important part of his stage act that made him so exciting to see.

Melvin Davis, "Detroit's Soul Ambassador," when interviewed, talked about how he followed Jackie Wilson heavily during his heyday at local Detroit clubs such as the Graystone Ballroom on Woodward Avenue, which had a "great dance floor."

Davis said, "Jackie would have singing fits. He was a chosen vessel. He was like an evangelist. It was like the spirit would take over. … Jackie didn't have to dance when he came on stage with a cigarette. He threw it up in the air, dropped to his knees, got up, caught it, threw it down and stomped it out. … Jackie was a vessel and tool that the music chose!

He was a song stylist. He had impeccable timing. If Jackie Wilson were a car, he would be a Rolls-Royce, top of the line model. His physique was fit. … He was clean and prepared … an in-shape as a tack … superior confidence … He owned the stage. He was a badass."

Jackie also was soon to be discovered. Johnny Otis, who discovered many R&B artists during the 1950s, claimed to have done the same for Jackie at an amateur night at the Paradise Theater.

He remembers one week where Jackie came in third place to Little Willie John and Levi Stubbs, and Otis gave himself credit for "discovering" Jackie. Through conversations and memories of different associates and friends, he did not.

Once Jackie was discovered, there was no looking back for him. Johnny Otis wanted him to join a group called the Thrillers. Jackie knew them all well but he didn't sing with them.

Around 1950, the group was renamed, calling themselves the Royals. It included Levi Stubbs, Lawson Smith, "Sonny" Woods, Henry Booth and Charles Sutton with Alonzo Tucker on guitar. Levi Stubbs stated that his cousin Jack had a bad ass voice.

In 1951, 17-year-old Jackie met up with guitarist Billy Davis, then 13, and Jackie was like a big brother to him. Billy's and Jackie's parents were all from Mississippi. "Our mothers knew each other from Mississippi because they lived near each other," says Davis. "They both worked at the same place picking cotton."

Jackie's parents moved north first. Then Davis' parents moved north, and the boys met up again at that point. When Davis was asked about his impression of Jackie Wilson, he had this to say, "He was more like an adult. He was more mature, beyond his young age. His greatest passion in life was singing."

When Davis was asked about Alonzo Tucker he recalled, "He was a songwriter from the old school. Tucker taught us a lot about R&B, how to write a song, have a concept, create a title."

Tucker and Jackie became very close friends, and Jackie was to record more compositions by Tucker than any other songwriter. Jackie would also co-write numerous tunes with him. They remained close throughout Jackie's entire career.

The originals group, "The Midnighters," consisted of Henry Booth, Lauren Smith, Sonny Wood, and lead singer Charlie Sutton. Later, they would evolve into the R&B group called "Hank Ballard and the Midnighters," but Jackie was not a part of the group they changed their name and signed with King Records.

In 1952, while in Chicago, Jackie met his lifelong friend and god sister Lena (Beasley) Towner when he was 18. Young Lena was around 15 herself working with disc jockey Sam Evans on his radio show *Jam with Sam.* Lena remembers when Jackie made an appearance at her school with Evans and she grabbed a personal belonging of Jackie's and ran into the girl's bathroom.

But Jackie ran after her but, to her surprise, when he caught up with her, he was neither angry nor upset. He was a perfect gentleman. In fact, he became a big brother figure from that day forward because he recognized that she needed someone to look out for her. Lena stated she went on to work with Chess Records and kept in touch with Jackie over the years.

Some of the great things she said about him were that he was "a kind person ... cool to talk to ... the same off stage as he was on stage ... humble and very down to earth."

46

Sugar Ray Robinson and Jackie Wilson

Towner told us that the radio show *Jam with Sam,* was broadcasted out of Gary, Indiana, and was owned by Mr. and Mrs. Carl Carter. Sam Evans was the disc jockey for the program, which was broadcast from the second floor of the South Center department store on 47th Street in Chicago.

Leonard Chess, owner of Chess Records, and Evans were promoting Jackie Wilson's and fellow boxer-turned— singer Sugar Ray Robinson's music.

They brought Jackie and Robinson to her school, DuSable High School in Chicago, to promote their singles.

Around that time, singers LaVern Baker, Little Willie John, Johnnie Ray and Della Reese were managed by Al Green, not to be confused with R&B singer Al Green nor Albert "Al" Green of the now defunct National Records. Green owned the music publishing companies Merrimac Music and Pearl Music, as well as Detroit's Flame Show Bar in Paradise Valley, where Jackie met Lavern Baker and they recorded together.

Al Green was the one who gave Berry a chance and the opportunity to write songs for Jackie. Although Berry Gordy had not yet founded Motown Records, he was a gifted songwriter. Berry would later pen and co-write hits for Jackie, including his first hits, "Reet Petite," "Lonely Teardrops," and "To Be Loved."

Jackie first recorded in Detroit at United Sound Systems Recording Studios as "Sonny" Wilson. He recorded for Dizzy Gillespie's Dee Gee Records in sessions produced by David Usher. The songs he cut included "Danny Boy" and "Rainy Day Blues."

In 1953, Jackie was told about an upcoming audition with Billy Ward, to replace Clyde McPhatter, of the Dominoes. He was so excited that he went around the neighborhood talking about it. When he went and told Mr. Wilson Boyd, he told Jackie, "Man, you have to be sharp." Mr. Wilson told my brother Tony and me, "I gave your father a crispy white shirt and nice tie to audition in." Jackie was successful in his audition to replace the immensely popular Clyde McPhatter, who left the Dominoes and formed his own group, the Drifters.

Mama Freda said that Jackie almost blew his chance that day, showing up calling himself "The Shit" Wilson and bragging about being a better singer than McPhatter. He was really feeling himself. Billy Ward felt that his new member needed a stage name to fit his Dominoes' image. Hence, Sonny was now called, "Jackie Wilson."

Prior to leaving the Dominoes, McPhatter coached Jackie on the sound Billy Ward wanted for his group, influencing Jackie's singing style and stage presence. Jackie said, "I learned a lot from Clyde," he later recalled, "That high-pitched choke he used, and other things ... Clyde McPhatter was my man."

Jackie was their lead singer for three years, but the Dominoes lost some of their stride with the departure of McPhatter. They were able to make appearances riding on the strength of the group's earlier hits until 1956 when an unlikely interpretation of the pop hit, "St. Therese of the Roses" gave the Dominoes another brief moment in the spotlight.

Their only other post-McPhatter/Wilson successes were "Stardust," released July 15, 1957, and "Deep Purple," released Oct. 7, 1957.

In 1957, Jackie set out to begin a solo career, leaving the Dominoes and collaborating with his cousin Levi Stubbs. When Levi began as the lead singer for the "Four Tops." He got work at Detroit's Flame Show Bar. Later, Al Green worked out a deal with Decca Records, and Jackie was signed to their subsidiary label, Brunswick Records.

Shortly after Jackie signed a solo contract with Brunswick, Green died suddenly and Green's business partner, Nat Tarnopol, took over as Jackie's manager. Tarnopol was the pioneer of Brunswick Records. He later rose to president of the company with Jackie's first single, "Reet Petite," which was a smash hit. The song was written by another former boxer, Berry Gordy Jr., with writing partner Roquel "Billy" Davis (not to be confused with Jackie's friend, guitarist Billy Davis) and Gordy's sister Gwendolyn.

The trio composed and produced six further singles for Jackie: "To Be Loved," "I'm Wanderin'," "We Have Love," "That's Why (I Love You So)," "I'll Be Satisfied" and his late-1958 signature song, "Lonely Teardrops," which peaked at No. 7 on the pop charts and No. 1 on the R&B charts in the U.S. and established him as an R&B superstar.

With the success of "Lonely Teardrops," he became known for his extraordinary, operatic multi-octave vocal range. The single sold more than one million copies and was awarded a gold disc by the Recording Industry Association of America (RIAA).

When (Sonny) now Jackie was on the road, he and his guitarist Billy Davis, while traveling on the road, would often eat at local diners and order the same food to eat, especially pancakes because Billy and Jackie were as close as brothers could be. They would talk about any and everything over the days on the road, from UFOs to comic books. Jackie was such a comic fan, he loved Thor especially and named his son Thor after the character.

When Jackie performed, with his dynamic dance moves, singing and impeccable dress, he was soon christened, "Mr. Excitement," a title he would keep for the remainder of his career. His stagecraft in his live shows inspired James Brown, Michael Jackson and Elvis Presley, as well as a host of other artists.

Jackie broke racial barriers because when he sang no one saw color. He was able to adapt to different cultural environments and had many friends, including Debbie Reynolds and Elvis Presley.

Elvis Presley admired Jackie so much. He first saw him perform in 1956 as lead singer with Billy Ward and the Dominos in Las Vegas.

Jackie was godfather to the American singer and songwriter, Jody Watley. As I said, Presley was so impressed with Jackie that he made it a point to meet him. The two instantly became good friends. In a photo of the two posing together, Presley's caption in the autograph reads, "You got a friend for life." Jackie also said he was influenced by Presley. Elvis and Jackie were only six months apart in age.

Elvis and Jackie were great friends, and they had a lot of things in common: They both had similar musical roots, having begun singing gospel and, most of all, each had a deep love for and bond with their mothers. Elvis and Jackie had great respect for each other.

Jackie's powerful, electrifying and dynamic live performances rarely failed to bring audiences into a state of frenzy. As he would perform, women would throw their underwear on stage, cry and pass out.

When he hit the stage and sang, his live performances consisted of knee-drops, splits, spins, back-flips, as well as removing his tie and jacket and throwing them off the stage. He also incorporated a lot of basic boxing steps such as his crossover skip as one of his favorite routines, getting girls in the audience to come up and kiss him and he would come out on stage smoking a cigarette, Du Maurier cigarettes, a special imported brand from Imperial Tobacco Canada.

He would start the intro to a song, throw the cigarette up in the air, drop into a split, jump back and catch the cigarette, and never lose a beat.

Jackie and Billy Davis

CHAPTER SIX

Billy Davis: Lifelong Friend

Guitarist Billy Davis, my father's lifelong friend and a Rock & Roll Hall of Fame inductee, told me, "Jackie and I were childhood friends. You can say we were family. I started playing for Jackie in the 1950s. I started traveling and continued playing for him from the 1960s through 1974."

Billy said he and Jackie would get up and have a shot early in the morning before they went to breakfast.

When touring, as they rode to the next town, Jackie and Billy had many conversations. Some were about UFOs. Jackie would read his Marvel comic books and buy them whenever he could on the road. It was hard touring the "chitlin' circuit."

Billy said Jackie barely had a normal life because he had management constantly telling him what to do and August, who worked for the mob, was his overseer. Billy's statement was confirmed in the book, "Jackie Wilson: The Man, the Music, the Mob," by Tony Douglas.

Following is an excerpt from that book:

"*Tommy Vastola and Johnny Roberts replaced Nat Tarnopol as Jackie's personal manager. Johnny Roberts hired August Sims who was a Black bodyguard for the legendary Middle Weight Boxer Sugar Ray Robinson. Sims met Roberts in 1963; as a matter of fact, Roberts and Jackie both wanted Sims to work with them. Sims job was to protect Jackie, keep up with the money and make sure the money was sent to them every time Jackie performed. However, the main thing Sims was to do was to make sure Jackie was doing what he was supposed to do and that was to perform and make them the money. Sims got rid of all of the blood sucking people Jackie had around him like best friend JJ. Sims told Jackie they were all just using him and the white mother fucker too. Jackie seemed not to care or believe it. He just wanted to sing. Sims toured with Jackie for a decade.*"

August Sims
and Jackie

Brenda
2 years old

Continuing, Billy also shared that, "Jackie would always talk about his children, and whenever they were in the audience, how he called them on stage. He didn't like the fact his management controlled his life and he was really upset when they kept him away from his children. He didn't like that at all."

Billy reminisces about how he met Brenda. "I remember Jackie told me to come over to his mother's, Eliza Mae's, house. He said that he had a surprise for me. When I got there, Jackie's mother was preparing dinner. I saw Jackie sitting down holding Brenda on his lap. She was a pretty baby girl who looked about two years old. Jackie said to me, 'This is my baby girl, Brenda.' On many occasions, Jackie had always acknowledged Brenda from birth as his biological daughter. I remember personally having seen them together more than once. His mother, Eliza, sister Joyce and other family members were there at the house. I know that 1967 was the last time I saw Jackie and Brenda together.

Billy Davis said during Jackie Wilson's performance at Houston's City Auditorium, "He walked on stage and opened his mouth ... just a kiss, just a smile, that's all I need." Then the crowd would go wild. "Hank Ballard and the Midnighters," LaVern Baker, "The Flamingos" and Sam Cooke were all there; suddenly the crowd rushed the stage, causing law officials to end the show. The Fire Marshall said it was too dangerous for the show to continue. Just like that the show was over. It happened in Fresno, California around 1960. Jackie was the hottest artist in the country at the time. The law officers had to use fire hoses to tame the wild crowd because Jackie and his entourage could not get out of there.

Billy told me that when Jackie came back from singing with The Dominoes he was ready to start his solo career. He was looking for Berry so he went to Berry's sister Gwen's house on Hague Street where she had a piano. Jackie wanted Berry to do some songs for him. Uncle Billy says he has a tape of Berry playing, "Lonely Teardrops," and "To Be Loved," on the piano before they recorded it at Bristoe Bryant's studio on East Grand Boulevard in Detroit. Jackie was the vocalist and Berry and his writing team wrote the songs.

Jackie also became a regular on television, making him a trailblazer at a time when blacks were rarely seen on TV. He performed his hits on such shows as *The Dick*

Clark Saturday Night Beechnut Show in 1960, *The Ed Sullivan Show* from 1960 to 1963, and *Shindig!* in 1964 and 1965. He made his one and only movie appearance, courtesy of Brunswick Records, in 1960's *Go, Johnny, Go!* In the film, he performed his song "You Better Know It." In 1971 he appeared on *The Jerry Lee Lewis Show* and in 1975 on PBS' *Soundstage* on WTTW Chicago.

This is a story told to me by Billy Davis that I thought was very interesting about Jackie.

Billy said, "In 1959, and in the 60's, we were touring with Supersonic Attractions, produced by Henry Wen. I was playing lead guitar with Hank Ballard and the Midnighters. I remember we were doing shows at that time with Bill Murray, who was also known in Detroit as 'Wine Head Willie.'

Then he started emceeing for Supersonic Attractions. That's when he started using his real name, 'Bill Murray.' When we started the tours, they would last at least 30 days. Bill Murray and I had a lot of conversations and he told me this one story about Jerry Lee Lewis.

Lewis was not supposed to be on the tour but Henry added him to the tour anyway. Bill said, 'They done added Jerry Lee Lewis to cover the last week of the tour to try to get Jerry to upset Jackie's appeal to the people. When Jerry did the show, he couldn't outdo Jackie Wilson. He was still kicking behinds on all the shows.

"There was a show on the East Coast. We did it in the summer in Charlotte, North Carolina and Richmond, Virginia. Bill Murray said to me, 'Billy, Jackie was the s***. Couldn't nobody come behind him, but we put Jerry Lee Lewis to come behind Jackie just before the shows. Yeah, we did it but it didn't work. After Jackie got finish, the show was over for Jackie. No one could follow him.

"I can't remember exactly where we were at this time, but Bill Murray when he started to introduce Jackie he said, 'Now I present to you the Crown Prince of Rock and Roll, Mister Jackie Wilson."

"Now, people started saying, 'Oh, that's a good name.'

"Everyone already felt that Jackie should have been called the 'King of Rock and Roll.'"

Jackie Wilson Tour Bus

Billy Davis recounted being "pissed off" about the things that were happening with Jackie. Jackie was reserved in his demeanor. One time in Newark, New Jersey, a strong-arm man named August Sims grabbed Jackie.

Billy stepped in and was ready to defend Jackie because he saw the fear in Jackie's eyes. Jackie told Billy to "Back off," and that Sims worked for the mob. The reason that Sims grabbed Jackie is because they had a heated argument about who had the most money: Howard Hughes or Frank Sinatra.

In 1961, in the Sire Arms Apartments in Manhattan, New York, on Valentine's Day, a woman whom we knew as Juanita Jones was waiting for Jackie and his girlfriend at that time to return from a date. Jones had a gun. When Jackie saw the gun, he began to wrestle with her to take the gun away. While they were wrestling, three shots were fired. Jackie got hit twice. One bullet in his left kidney and the second bullet near his spine.

He was rushed to the hospital and had immediate surgery. His left kidney was damaged and they removed it. He had to live with the bullet near his spine for the rest of his life.

This was told to me by Billy Davis and it's also in the book by Tony Douglas, "Jackie Wilson: The Man, the Music, the Mob."

Four years later, in 1967, Jackie got married but Billy Davis says Jackie was heartbroken. He quotes Jackie as saying, "I love her, but I can't live with her." They later obtained an official separation.

Baby Brenda

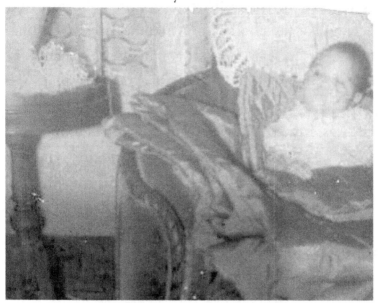

Brenda's graduation picture in Cap and Gown

CHAPTER SEVEN

Brenda: "To Be Loved"

Papa was a rolling stone. Susie was not the only one Jackie was involved with at that time. Although her circumstances were not favorable due to her pregnancy, she didn't allow her circumstances to determine the outcome of her unborn child, Brenda.

Like I said, I was born in Herman Kiefer Hospital; the same place as my dad. When my mother brought me home from the hospital, she lived at 568 Hague and John R. Street on the North End of Detroit. Susie was around in the early days when Sonny (aka Jackie) was boxing and she didn't really believe he would become famous as a singer. But she loved him regardless of what he said or did.

She made sure that her baby girl was taken care of. We lived with Uncle Bud and Auntie Margaret, who were her support system and they kept us sheltered.

Jackie stayed with Eliza Mae, Mama Freda, and the family and, as it has been stated, "He didn't deny any of his children." Susie would allow Jackie to take me to his house, and sometimes she would even visit. I always wonder where my nickname "Peanut" came from later on in my life. I found out that Daddy called me, "Peanut."

My mother was a very private person and a tough cookie. In other words, Susie didn't take no mess! She never applied for child support. She never asked for anything from Jackie. She let me know and see my father and family, as stated earlier. She understood and respected that Daddy married Mama Freda. Susie's focus was to raise me. She kept me in church and instilled in me family values. The scripture that comes to mind is, *"Train up a child in the way he should go, and even when he is old, he will not depart from it"* (Proverbs 22:6). Susie did just that.

Susie was a loving, God-fearing woman with a lot of integrity. I always felt so loved. She provided for me and made sure I was well taken care of. My earliest memories of my childhood start at age three. I remember being at my grandmother Eliza Mae's house with my Aunt Joyce, who was so sweet to me. I can remember standing outside the house on Cottage Grove Street and how Joyce would play with me. There was another baby in the house. Of course, I knew it was my sister. Back then it was a happy time and safe place for me. I felt so much love from both homes: my grandmother Eliza Mae's house and mine.

Some of the things I remember from back then were going to the movie house on Oakland and Holbrook Avenues. Another time, my mother took me to the boxing gym to visit.

Being around my father, my grandmother, Auntie Joyce, Mama Freda and the kids when I was a young child, as I said, brought me great joy and lasting memories.

As my father became more popular, and I got older, I did not visit the family as much and then the visits stopped. My father, Jackie, was working towards his career to be a superstar now and no longer lived in Detroit.

He was touring with the group Billy Ward and His Dominoes. I learned the significance of my father being Jackie Wilson. I realized how great he was around the time I was in sixth grade. Most of all, I realized who I was, being fully aware of my ability to dance and sing. My talent was recognized by my teacher who pushed me to sing.

MY SCHOOL YEARS

Growing up, I knew I could sing. I had an operatic voice. My mother could sing. However, most of all, she taught me how to love and treat people the way I wanted to be treated, "To Be Loved."

My sixth-grade teacher, Ms. Antonovich, really took an interest in me and recognized my gift. She asked me to sing, "The Lord's Prayer," for our sixth-grade graduation, which I did. She called Mr. Breman, the high school music teacher for glee club and choir and told him she had someone who she really thought needed to be involved in those school vocal groups. She told him I could really sing and I had a beautiful voice. From the time she made the call, I was involved in singing, from sixth to 12th grade.

I was very involved in school activities. I started a singing group with three other girls. My chorus Teacher Mr. Breman, told me he thought I was the best vocalist in the school choir and asked me to sing the lead on the song "Summertime" for our Hamtramck High School spring concert. I did. In my senior year, I was voted best dancer for my senior class and was known as the best dancer in Hamtramck. I was a cheerleader and played on the varsity field hockey team and Junior Basketball team. I was very outgoing and active.

As I was growing up, I had many thoughts about music and dance. It was like my spirit and soul always knew that music was a dominant part of me. I told my mother that I wanted to be a professional dancer. "No, you're not doing that," she told me. "People don't make money dancing." We know that's not true today. But, back then, times were a little different. Motown was my era, growing up with the Motown sound. As my years progressed, you will see I was always thinking outside the box!

The year I graduated, 1967, was the same year my dad married his second wife, a model. When Jackie was in Detroit, he came to visit me at my home. My mother knew I would be surprised when she called out to me. "Brenda, come downstairs. Someone is here to see you." When I saw my father standing in my living room, my heart skipped a beat and my eyes lit up. It was Jackie Wilson, my daddy, in the flesh. When we saw each other he said, "You have turned out to be so beautiful." We hugged each other. That was such a precious moment for me. He asked me if I wanted to go for a ride in the limo. Enthusiastically, I responded, "Yes, of course!"

We were in the car laughing, talking and, with a lot of hugs, we were having a wonderful time and conversation. He asked me how I was doing and what my plans were since graduation. I shared with him what my dreams were and that I was not completely sure what I wanted to pursue as my life's profession.

He told me, "You will figure it out, and I am very proud of you. Susie did a very good job raising you. I love you and I loved your mom."

From our conversation, I believe he wanted his children to be able to work together in harmony and love one another. He showed me a lot of love in the times I spent with him. Though it all, my mom told me who my father was.

After graduation, I continued singing in both a gospel and secular group. We hung out at Golden World Records on Davison Street, which was owned by Ed Wingate. There were a lot of other recording artists there, including the Dramatics. Our girls group recorded some background vocals on some songs.

Loving Memories of My Mother Susie

Thinking about my mother, Susie, I remember her as a woman of integrity, insight and love. She took very good care of me and my children. She lived her life for God and our Lord Jesus Christ. Susie was always in church singing. She sang at homegoings at James Cole's funeral home. My mother was a giving person and a blessing to others.

Upon her illness, she told me it was all on me now. It was all on me to pray, live a godly life, and walk in integrity. She instilled in me to help as many people as I could and serve God. She passed away on Aug. 10, 2007, at age 80.

Her homegoing was held at Leland Missionary Baptist Church on Fenkell Avenue in Detroit, where she had been a member for more than 55 years. She was laid to rest at Detroit Memorial Park. I love, Mom, and I will always remember your love for me and for others.

Mama Freda

I often reminisce about the times I spent with Mama Freda ...

In the 1990s, I would visit her frequently in her apartment on Glendale Avenue in Highland Park, and she would show me pictures and tell me stories. The first time that I walked into her apartment I saw an armoire filled with pictures and whatnots. One of the photos looked like me! When I asked where she got my picture?

"Brenda, that's not you," she said. "That's Sandy. You guys look so much alike. You have the same eyes and nose." I said, "Dang, that looks just like me." She said, "I know."

Mama Freda would call me all the time at my office at WMKM, a gospel radio station, almost every other day. I was the general sales manager. I can remember having a conversation with her in 1992 when I was doing the Apollo-style talent showcase at the Latin Quarter.

Mama Freda told me a story about how the mob took care of my daddy; how they would give him money, limos and other things.

She said Jackie trusted them and that Brunswick artists had been defrauded of their royalties. She also told me that because I was Jackie Wilson's daughter, "I should be looking out." And I said, "Looking out for what?"

She responded, "Looking out for them because one day they are going to show up."

Still puzzled, I asked, "Who's going to show up?"

Mama Freda answered, "The men in the suits with the ponytails and a suitcase."

"Oh … O.K."

And then, amazingly, these men showed up at one of my talent shows. Not saying it was the mob. But following the show at the Latin Quarters I went to the Hotel Pontchartrain in Downtown Detroit, while I was there enjoying myself a Hostess from the hotel came and found me in the ballroom. She asked "are you Miss Wilson?"

I answered, "Yes."

"There are some men that would like to see you. I will take you to them." Directly outside the ballroom door, lo and behold, there were the two guys

Mama Freda told me about and had described to me. They had the ponytails, suits and a briefcase. I walked over to them.

They introduced themselves and invited me to have a seat. At that point they said, "We know who you are, and we would like to know if there is anything we can help you with?"

I was so surprised, cautious and a little fearful. I said to myself, how did these guys know where I was? I answered, "I don't know."

One of the gentlemen gave me his card and said, "If you think of anything, give us a call."

Now I am not saying that they were mob-affiliated or had any ties to a mob. It could just been a coincidence that they looked similar to the description Mama Freda gave me.

So, the next day, I called Mama Freda and told her, "Sho' nuf" the guys in the suits with the ponytails and briefcases showed up.

She started laughing and said, "I told you they would because you are Jackie Wilson's daughter."

Unfortunately, death struck the family, and Mama Freda asked me to sing at the homegoing of the baby of her granddaughter, my niece. When I arrived for the service on Oakland Avenue, I did not know how the baby, my grandniece, had passed.

When I found out the cause was Sudden Infant Death Syndrome (SIDS), I was overcome with grief, because I had experienced the same tragedy with the loss of my son from SIDS, and the memory was too great. I could not sing so I left.

The next day, I called Mama Freda and explained what had happened and why I could not sing. I told her that I had the same experience. I had a baby boy who died of SIDS and that it brought back too many sad memories.

"Why didn't you tell me?" she said. "I really understand." She was not upset with me because that just was the way Mama Freda was. As I said earlier, her words were full of compassion and love.

Mama Freda would call me regularly up until the time of her death in July of 1999. I was in Missouri at the time working for the church's summer youth camp. The day I returned from youth camp someone called me at the church to give me her condolences for the passing of my mother.

I told her that my mother didn't pass. I had no idea that she was saying Mama Freda had passed. Then she said, "Freda Wilson," who was a mother at the church. I was shocked that Mama Freda had passed. I was devastated, knowing I was not able to attend her homegoing. I loved her very much. She treated me like a daughter.

My mother, Susie, and Mama Freda knew each other, and they knew a lot of the same people. Mama Freda knew me and accepted me as Jackie's daughter. She would tell me stories about my father. Mama Freda has always mention me in her interview for the books about Jackie Wilson written by Tony Douglas.

I remember one time taking my mother and Mama Freda to a court appointment.

As we were riding, they were reminiscing about Jackie and the people they knew. They were talking about the good times they had back in the day. I loved these two mothers.

Jackie watching himself on Ed Sullivan Show

CHAPTER EIGHT

The Decline of Jackie Wilson "Stop Doggin' Me Around"

In 1958, Billy Roquel Davis and Berry Gordy left Jackie and Brunswick after royalty disputes escalated between them and management. It had been rumored that the artist was being mismanaged. There were also allegations of money laundering and blood ties (rumored Mafia involvement). It was said that there were two sets of books. While Jackie was selling millions of records worldwide, he was only getting paid for less than half of what he earned.

In a *20/20* interview, songwriter Al Kasha stated that he was a friend of my father and that Jackie Wilson and other songwriters were being cheated out of royalties.

Also, that management was taking credit for songs they never wrote or had no involvement in at all. Jackie trusted his management. He and his manager left Detroit and moved to New York in 1961.

Jackie just wanted to sing. He left all the management to his manager. It is said that the mob muscled their way into the business and put a guy out on the road with Jackie to keep him in line and to keep track of the money. They were Mr. first August Sims and Johnny Roberts.

Billy Roquel Davis was signed to Chess Records as a producer and staff songwriter. He found success in songwriting. While Gordy ventured out on his own and founded Motown Records, located at the Hitsville U.S.A. studio on Detroit's west side. Because of Jackie's operatic vocal range, management was convinced that Jackie, "Mr. Excitement," could make it as a successful solo artist.

In 1957, it was arranged for Jackie to work with Decca Records' veteran arranger Dick Jacobs. Jackie scored continuous hits during the 1950s and in the 1960s rolled in with the number one single, "Doggin' Around," and the soulful song, "Night."

Jackie was a top hit-maker with songs such as "Baby Workout" and turned out other songs, including "No Pity (In the Naked City)" and, "I'm So Lonely." Jackie continued to tour around the country, and at one venue down in New Orleans in 1960, the crowd was so out of control that police had to surround the stage.

One of Jackie's fans, as they always did, tried to rush the stage and was pushed down. Jackie's mutual love and respect for his fans kicked in, and he assaulted the police officer. He was arrested for defending his fans. Lena Towner, his god sister, asked him why he allowed his fans to come backstage and carry on the way they do, he replied, "I love my fans."

From 1964 to 1966, Wilson's career had also hit an all-time slump but Jackie continued to record with musical legends to add another notch in his belt, including jazz great Count Basie, R&B star LaVern Baker, and blues and gospel singer Linda Hopkins.

In 1966, things began to look up when he scored the first of two big comeback singles hits with an established producer out of Chicago, Carl Davis, "Whispers (Gettin' Louder)" and "(Your Love Keeps Lifting Me) Higher and Higher."

Playing Bass guitar was James Jamerson, A key to his musical rebirth was Carl Davis. Although, it was alleged that he was urged to leave his record company to head over to Motown, Jackie resisted. It was a decision that may have forever changed the trajectory of events in the remaining years of Jackie's life and career.

I was given my father's wallet at the street dedication in 2016. That's when I discovered that in 1969, while Jackie was living in New York, that he was the President of Novel Production, Inc, on Purchase Street in Purchase, New York.

The company purchased a 1969 Gold Cadillac Sedan and the New York Department of Motor Vehicles issued Sticker No. 334959 on March 3, 1969. He also had a Western Union receipt for $750.00 dollars to pay one month rent at 155 68th Street in New York, New York for his second wife. He apparently stayed at 35 East Dorchester Towers and listed Brunswick Record's address as 455 Park Avenue.

In the 1970s, there was a family tragedy. Jackie Jr. was shot and passed away and Sandra passed in 1977 of a heart attack. Jacqueline died in 1988 but daddy didn't know about his daughters' deaths because he was in the nursing home from 1975 to 1984. Jackie Wilson was one of the remaining artists on the Brunswick record label and continued to record with them but found no significant pop chart success. The Internal Revenue Service later indicted its top executive for fraud.

Actually, because of his mismanagement, Jackie also owed the IRS more than $300,000 and they wanted to know why taxes had not been paid. It's unfortunate that someone allegedly made a choice to make the fruits of Jackie's labor their own and chose not to share with him or to allow him to profit from his decades of hard work.

When Jackie was performing with the Dick Clark's Good Ol' Rock and Roll Revue in Cherry Hill, New Jersey, in September 1975, he was scheduled to testify to the IRS about taxes concerning Brunswick recording company. He was supposed to have owned half in Chicago while Nat Tarnopol owned the one in New York. Jackie was paid in cash and the IRS wanted to know why taxes had not been paid.

Jackie was going to testify against his management around the time of his performance for Dick Clark's revue in New Jersey. Somehow, he never made it because he collapsed on stage during the show.

He had a heart attack, fell and hit his head. He was admitted to Cherry Hill Hospital in New Jersey. His brain was swollen to the point of inducing a coma. He was defibrillated six times in emergency and three times in the coronary care unit. The bottom line is that the patient was not able to talk or understand verbal or written language. They did try to save Jack and he stayed in the nursing home for nine years. He never got to testify, so the truth was never revealed.

In September 1975, God wasn't ready for Jackie Wilson to come home yet. He spent eight and a half years in a comatose state. Technology was not available back then as it is today to find out what caused his heart attack.

Following is an eye-witness report of Jackie's last performance.

"Hi I'm Dr. Delores Brown telling the story to Brenda Wilson, Jackie's daughter. "Yes, I would tell you it was 1975. I remember it was in September it was cool. I live in Willingboro, New Jersey. Your father was performing at the Latin Casino in Cherry Hill, New Jersey. My sister Diane (who is deceased now) wanted to take me out because my youngest son was two years old and I had not

really been out. She knew that I always played a lot of Jackie Wilson, the Four Tops and The temptations. I love music. So did Diane. We got dressed in our little go-go boots, hats and everything; and we went to the Latin Casino. The place was packed, Brenda. Diane and I were seated at the fourth table from the front of the stage. It was a very good feeling. Another group, The Coasters, also performed; but I went basically to see your father.

"When he came out on stage, he was like skipping and happy to be out there. And, if I remember, I think he had on a leather pants suit with some designs on the top. The one song that I wanted him to sing was 'Lonely Teardrops.' And that was the last song he sang before he collapsed.

"When he finished singing, he thanked all of us for coming and said something to the effect that he loved us. He appreciated us, and he held his arm up, made a fist and said, 'Power to the people.' I remember that, 'Power to the people.,' And then he turned.

"Everything just went wild. He had fallen and, as far I can see, the gentleman came out who is trying to work with them there on the floor. I was told later the man was one *of The Coasters. They immediately started getting us out of there and everything but that is what I can recall.*

"I thank the Lord that I did see it.

"Someone said that Dick Clark was there, but I didn't see him. People were standing up and everything and I really couldn't see that well. People started talking among themselves. They were asking, 'What happened?' 'What happened? What's going on?' And then the security people came to get us out. When The Coaster guy, Cornelius Gunther, came out, it looked like he was doing CPR mouth to mouth.

"Because I had a good table, I could see. I was on the far right, on the end, so I could see him when he ran out on stage. I had a great seat when the gentleman was trying to work on your dad. He kept leaning down, you know, trying to talk to him. Probably saying something like, 'Hold on,' something to that effect.

"When I turned to leave everyone else had come up to try to see what was happening on stage. Everything happened so fast. It kind of caught you off-guard as to what you saw and what you didn't see.

"All I can really recall is what he said to us and that he didn't stumble walking out there like people are saying that he had a heart attack or something like that. He didn't look sick. He was able to finish performing 'Lonely Teardrops,' the last song he ever sang and he finished the whole song. 'Thank you for coming,' he said to us, raising his fist, and saying, 'Power to the people.'

"And then he turned and the next thing I know there were a lot of people in front of me. But I can see enough to know he had fallen. So we left the Latin Casino and, as we were riding, we didn't hear anything on the radio when we were going across the Walton Whitman Bridge about what had happened. It was really an eerie thing.

"We were listening to R&B stations and so forth, but nothing was said. It was the next day before they said anything. Then they didn't say he had a heart attack. I don't know when I started hearing that. It was just said something to the effect that he had taken ill at the Latin Casino in New Jersey. That's what they said. They didn't go into detail or anything about what had happened."

CHAPTER NINE

Sickness, Death, Funeral

No More, No More, Lonely Teardrops

Dick Clark's Good Ol' Rock and Roll Revue— Cherry Hill, N.J.

In 1975, Jackie's mother, Eliza Mae, made it to the hospital to see her only son. After six weeks, the Cherry Hill Medical Center had done all they could to help my father, and he was put into Medford Leas nursing home in Medford, New Jersey. For nine years, my father lived in that nursing home. Our once vibrant and show-stopping father was reduced to a comatose state. My father would never want to live if he could not sing. That was his purpose in life: sing and bring joy and happiness to his family, fans and friends.

Gone Home to Glory

My father's death on Jan. 21, 1984, was a heavy blow to the hearts of people around the world. Jackie Wilson was a light gone out at 49.

The homegoing was at Russell Street Baptist Church. His lifelong friends Berry Gordy was in attendance. B.B King, James Brown and Aretha Franklin were scheduled to perform at a nightclub show in San Francisco. They all got together, including Berry Gordy Jr., and sent a beautiful floral arrangement of a record with a picture of a young Jackie with "Lonely Teardrops" in gold letters across the front of the reef. James Brown wrote on the card that came with the flowers, "There will never be another like this soul brother."

Brenda and the Funeral

I really wanted to attend the service, and I mustered up enough strength to drive to the church. When I pulled up in front of Russell Street Baptist Church, a man walked up to my car and told me that I had to move. I told him that I was the daughter of Jackie Wilson. He said, "Come on. I will take you in."

"Wait a minute, please." I needed a minute to get myself together; he gave me a moment and then he took me through the gated parking lot to the side door entrance and up to the sanctuary door.

I opened the door, looked in, saw all the people, and saw the casket. It was then that I felt the numbness. I was frozen and could not move. I looked again at the people, and I backed up to close the door. The gentleman was still standing by my side, and he said, "You going in?"

I said, "No, I can't. I don't want to see him like that, in a casket."

Really, I just wanted to remember him the way I last saw him: alive and smiling, riding around talking and laughing together, and him giving me a big hug and a kiss on my forehead as I got out of the limo, as my mother stood at the limo door saying her goodbyes to Jackie. That visit declared my father's love for me.

With the image of these memories in my head, I turned around, walked down the stairs, thanked the man, and went to my car, sat there for a moment and I left.

He was laid to rest at Westlawn Cemetery in Wayne,

Michigan. Initially, my father, Jackie Wilson, was buried in an unmarked grave. However, CBS Records executive LeBaron Taylor, who attended Jackie's 1987 Rock & Roll Hall of Fame induction ceremony, told pioneering radio personality

Jack Gibson (aka Jack the Rapper) about our father's situation. Gibson, one of the nation's first black disc jockeys and the editor of a music industry newsletter, started the Jackie Wilson Marker Fund the month he was inducted, in January 1987.

Gibson was the first to pledge $500 and ask his listeners and readers to do the same. Only $4,000 was needed to pay for the marker, but they raised $5,000. Jack stated that the fund was growing and that if it reached $10,000 by May, that our father and our grandmother could be laid to rest in a beautiful mausoleum.

Today, Jackie's mother's body is laid to rest next to her beloved son's. The money came from friends and fans all over the world.

The epitaph on the mausoleum gravestone reads, "And Now No More Lonely Teardrops" because mother and son are reunited for eternity.

The dedication took place on my father's 53rd birthday at his resting place, Westlawn Cemetery.

Looking back, my father's funeral was one of the hardest days of my life and it took a toll on my life for many years … "To Be Loved" by my father, who was gone, and who I would never see again. It wasn't easy to say goodbye, so I said, "'I'll Be Satisfied' with the memories I have of him and his legacy."

The road got rough, but God saved me for such a time as this—to keep my father's legacy and memory alive— And the Legacy Continues …

CHAPTER TEN

The Prayer Bench, Jackie Wilson Lane, The Family Speaks

A true legacy needed to be fulfilled. An heiress needed to accept her birthright and come to the throne of her father to continue his mission.

Brenda Wilson, daughter of "Mr. Entertainment," Jackie Wilson, knew she had to fulfill her destiny. She has taken the initiative to restore his name and keep his heritage alive.

Now the saga will continue with the memories and the talents of his daughter Brenda. She is the epitome of love.

Her heart is pure, and her wisdom is inspirational. She gradually accepted every challenge that was bestowed upon her. She is a natural, down-to-earth example of loving and respecting others.

Brenda is driven by her humanitarian nature to motivate, encourage and inspire others to be successful. For all who encounter her, she yearns to instill in them to use the God-given talent, which is in them.

Always striving to help others, she is a beacon of light, shining and casting a spiritual glow of hope to help people positively fulfill their own destinies, as well as her own.

In the past 30 years, Brenda has been an active participant and motivator in her community. As a mother of five (Roscoe, Alicia, Angelica, Lizzie and Erika), she values and supports the nurturing of today's youth and believes that the young people of today need more positive guidance.

Instead of killings, drugs, guns and violence, young people need to live peacefully, and she wants to help them grow up in the God given way and love one another.

Brenda's Children

Brenda's Grandchildren

Brenda's Great
Grandchildren

Brenda's daughter Erika is a psychiatric nurse, songwriter, singer with top—range vocals, a clothing designer and a hairstylist with an extensive management resume. She is also currently working toward becoming a nurse practitioner. Son, Roscoe, is a retired Master Sergeant of 29 years, nicknamed "Iron Man," who served in Desert Storm, Kosovo and Iraq. He is now a successful resident in Germany.

Angelica is in a high-ranking, city municipal position. Alicia is in city management and involved with other community events and school board involvements. Lizzie is a chef at a prestigious restaurant who is working toward owning her own business. Brenda has 12 grandchildren: Roscoe Jr., Ebony, Alexis, Malaysia, Micah, Alaya, Keyonna, Kyecia, Keith, Kenneth, Kevin and Jalen. She has three great-grandkids: Antonio, Autumn and Jacoby.

Brenda is so very proud of her children and grandchildren. Her grandson Roscoe has graduated from Michigan State University, and her granddaughter Micah attends the University of Michigan.

Keyonna, Alaya and Kyecia graduated from the prestigious Cass Technical High School. Keyonna attends Jackson State University in Mississippi, Alaya attends Western Michigan University in Kalamazoo, and Kyecia attends Wayne State University in Detroit. Her grandson Kenneth attends Ferris State University and Keith attended Olivet College, both in Michigan, while Kevin and Jalen are in high school.

She is a producer of various talent shows to highlight Detroit's budding talents such as the Apollo-style showcase, "Apollo: Live in Michigan," which is a platform for dancers, actors, comedians, singers and rappers. She is currently working for the Jackie Wilson Foundation, which she established in 2015.

The Granite Prayer Bench

Initiated in 1992 by Joseph "Jack the Rapper," Brenda was asked to assist him in putting together a program to dedicate a prayer bench to Jackie Wilson. He raised money to place an add on the Granite Prayer Bench in front of Jackie and Eliza Mae mausoleum with donations from Jackie Wilson fans. It is at Westlawn Cemetery in Wayne, Michigan. The bench has the words, "Jackie The Complete Entertainer" written on the front of it.

Jack The Rapper and Brenda Unveiling Prayer Bench

Brenda considers it an honor that Jack asked her to help him and was very happy to put the program together.

Brenda invited the Wilson family, along with Jack the Rapper, Ernie Durham, Marv Johnson, Freda Wilson, Reginal Abrams and Rev. Mikel Features. The program was a big success and the Granite Prayer Bench is there today for all family, friends, and fans to sit, meditate and reflect on their memories of "Mr. Excitement," the Great entertainer Jackie Wilson.

Again, words cannot express the feelings of gratitude Brenda has for Jack the Rapper for the love and respect he had for her father. Knowing he was buried in an unmarked grave, in 1987 he raised thousands of dollars to place him and his mother into a Mausoleum from donations from him, friends and fans.

Jackie Wilson Lane

In 2015, Brenda met with the Highland Park mayor at the time, Deandre Windom, along with Lamont Robinson and Cheryl Ruffin of the R&B Music Hall of Fame.

Lamont, Cheryl and Brenda supported each other in their endeavors. Mayor Windom said he agreed that it was a good idea to name a street after Jackie Wilson. Brenda waited for a couple of weeks, and did not see or hear from the mayor who was campaigning for reelection.

So, she contacted her friend Christopher Woodard, President of the Highland Park City Council, to get some advice or direction on whom she should be talking to and the protocol for getting the street-naming done.

On September 21, 2015, the Highland Park City Council convened at 7:09 p.m. with President Woodard presiding. Council members Norma Lewis, Mamie Posey Moore, Rodney Patrick and Titus McCalary were present. With a quorum, the council was declared in session.

According to the meeting minutes, "THEREFORE, BE IT RESOLVED that the Highland Park City Council hereby adopts and approves; moved by Council President Christopher Woodard and supported by Councilmember McCary, to rename Cottage Grove Street to Jackie Wilson Lane." Oh, what a happy day! Good news.

When Brenda got the call about the decision, she was so excited. The team felt they needed to celebrate the wonderful news with family, friends and fans. They were told and the celebration was on!

The first plan was to do the street renaming celebration on the actual street, Cottage Grove, but after Brenda did a site visit, she decided that it would not be a good idea because of the condition of the area and safety of the public that would be in attendance.

After the site visit, Brenda went to Plan B. She began to put the A team together. She also called family members Sabrina, Thor, Anthony and Reggie to tell them the wonderful news and about the plans for the celebration for the Jackie Wilson street renaming. Everyone was very excited about a street being named after Jackie Wilson.

Gisele Caver (aka Key of Gee) was the first person contacted. Then she called Pat Ford, Lizzie Johnson, Erika Johnson and Cheryl Ford. Maxine Willis of WHPR, Highland Park City Council President Christopher Woodard and Brenda met, and plans began to fall in place.

But first Brenda had to go to the City Council to share the plans to have a celebration. They quickly let her know that the city didn't have any money, so it was all on her.

Nevertheless, that wasn't going to stop the celebration. This was a big deal for the Wilson family. Brenda and her A team met, and plans began to take place.

Of course, there were some bumps in the road, but the date was set for Aug. 20, 2016, which turned out to be a great, blessed day.

During the time of planning the street naming ceremony, Brenda stayed in contact with her sister Sabrina. She was having some health challenges and told Brenda to tell everyone that she would not be in attendance because the doctor wouldn't release her to fly. However, Brenda did announce her well wishes.

Detroit Free Press

Highland Park Mayor Hubert Yopp (from left) and Jackie Wilson's children, Thor, Brenda, and Anthony Wilson, celebrate the renaming of Cottage Grove Street to Jackie Wilson Lane at a ceremony WHPR TV and radio studios in the city Saturday, Aug. 20, 2016. *Keith Matheny Free Press*

Howard Hertz, Brian Pastoria. Erika and Lizzie Johnson, Brenda Wilson and Mary Wilson of the Supremes

Brenda's brother Thor and his three children came from Atlanta, and her brother Anthony "Tony" Wilson was front and center with the rest of the Wilson family members all in attendance. Brenda was very happy to see all the hard work and effort the team did come to fruition — the family of entertainers.

On August 20, the place was filled with family and friends from all over the world: Mary Wilson of the Supremes was the keynote speaker; Bishop Rance Allen opened the program with prayer and a song, "Something About the Name Jesus;"

The Contours, the Stubbs Girls and Rob Carter all sang at the event. Reggie "Motsi Ski" Abrams of the famous rap group Detroit's Most Wanted also performed a wonderful tribute to his grandfather, Jackie Wilson.

RJ Watkins, owner and operator of WHPR TV and Radio Station, was very proud to be one of the sponsors of this great historic event held in his hometown, Highland Park.

The Jackie Wilson Foundation, Inc. and UAW Ford were major sponsors of the Jackie Wilson street naming at the studio filled with Highland Park's Mayor, the

Honorable Hubert Yopp, legendary Motown entertainers, national celebrities, dignitaries from the city of Highland Park, the city of Detroit, state of Michigan representatives and U.S. Congressman John Conyers.

Greg Dunmore of Pulsebeat did great interviews with all the celebrities in attendance.

The Wilson family members were all recognized for being in attendance for this historic evening. Brenda said she was so very overjoyed and in high spirits to see all the smiles and the happiness on all the faces. This tribute was an honor for all the family of the Legendary Jackie Wilson "Mr. Excitement."

Then came the unveiling of the street sign. On stage were Brenda Wilson, Anthony "Tony" Wilson and Thor Kenneth Wilson with Mayor Hubert Yopp.

Jackie Wilson Lane is now official, and it's a permanent street sign forever for all generations to see on Cottage Grove and Woodward Avenue.

Brenda attended the Jackie Wilson's name placement

on the first side of the historical markers at the famous United Sound Systems Recording Studios on June 25, 2017, located on Second Street in Detroit. His first recording was done there by Dizzy Gillespie's Dee Dee Records in a session produced by Dave Usher.

On June 9, 2018, UAW Ford and the Jackie Wilson Foundation sponsored a 2018 Black Music Month festival on the grounds of the Northwest Activities Center.

It was hosted by Brenda Wilson. In attendance were Jackie Wilson's son Anthony "Tony" Wilson, Jackie's sister Joyce Lee, her daughter Kelly Collins and Collins' father John Lee, along with many more Wilson family, friends and fans.

The festival included the Legend Tribute Concert and birthday celebration for Jackie Wilson featuring his grandson Reggie Abrams and Rob Carter.

Brenda Wilson performed a song by Motown legend Mary Wells, and there were tributes to other influential artists such as Prince by Simon Black, Louis Armstrong and James Brown by Braxton Davis, Jimi Hendrix by

Billy Davis, Isaac Hayes by El Shaw, the Supremes by Love Iam, Gladys Knight by Venus Ford, Teddy Pendergrass by Bubb Bear, Chuck Berry by Mighty Mick, Marvin Gaye by Jerry Brooks, and Michael Jackson by Tyuwan Brown.

There was a local talent showcase with a top-notch red carpet and VIP reception. This was a very successful event. The auditorium was filled with friend and fans.

No more lonely teardrops, NO MORE! NO MORE!

We shall cry, "NO MORE!"

The Family & Fans Speak!!!

He will live forever in our hearts, and his name will always be known globally.

Erika Johnson, granddaughter

"Mr. Excitement," Jackie Wilson was my inspiration to sing. I used to go and see him as a kid.

My mom took me to his shows, and I was electrified by his voice and showmanship. He was an inspiration to many world-renowned entertainers.

Simply stated, your dad was one of the best to ever do it. Congratulations on his star on the Hollywood Walk of Fame. Well-deserved and long overdue.

A lifelong fan

Brenda, I am so proud of you for keeping my god brother Jackie Wilson's legacy alive. I worked at Chess Records in those days in Chicago. I will be praying and believing for God's best for you. I hope that you will see your dreams come true.

Blessings, Lena Towers

Jackie Wilson was one of my greatest friends. His talent goes beyond his greatness and will last for generations.

I played his songs many, many times and still love them. I am proud of you, Brenda. Keep doing what you're doing. You have my support.

Love you always, Ken Bell

We would like to say that we are so proud of you and all your endeavors to keep your father and our grandfather's legacy alive.

It has been a long journey to get to this point in our lives. We love you. We appreciate you. May God continue to bless you and the works of your hands.

With love from your children,
Roscoe Johnson, Alicia Miller, Angelica Jones,
Lizzie Johnson and Erika Johnson.

My cousin, Jackie "Sonny" Wilson, was one of a kind. Not only was he a dynamic singer, he was a dynamic son to his mom, Aunt Eliza, and brother to his sister, Joyce, but also a loving father to his children. He was never too busy for his family.

He gave the world love through his melodious voice. Sonny, my brother Levi, and Little Willie John used to compete with each other in sing-offs at Detroit's Warfield Theater when they were teenagers before earning their fame.

Jackie, "Sonny," will forever be indelible in our hearts. His voice will never be silenced — just listen to his songs. May Cousin Jackie's voice ring forever.

With love, your cousin, Thelma Stubbs-Mitchell

In Conclusion

I hope you enjoyed the truths that I shared about my dad, Jackie Wilson. We knew him to be truly a loving man and a father and one of the greatest entertainers in the world.

There will never be another Jackie Wilson. He has been an inspiration to many, not only with his sound but also with his looks, his style and, most of all, the true love he had for his family, friends and fans. He made a lot of people happy all over the world. So, I guess he wasn't that bad of a person because right now, today, they are still playing his music; and he is still being recognized for the great entertainer he was.

He has his star in heaven, and now he will get his star on earth on September 4, 2019 on the Hollywood Walk of Fame.

WE LOVE YOU, JACK LEROY SONNY "JACKIE" WILSON, JR., MR. EXCITEMENT

Brenda and Jackie with Hollywood Walk of Fame Star

CHAPTER ELEVEN

Jackie Wilson's Accomplishments & Honors, 1987-2020

1987

- Inducted into the Rock & Roll of Hall of Fame in Cleveland, Ohio

- Inducted into the Michigan Doo-wop Hall of fame

1991 *(received posthumously by Brenda Wilson)*

- State of Michigan, Michigan Legislature House Resolution 306 H-Resolution of Tribute offered in memory of Jackie Wilson

1992 *(received posthumously by Brenda Wilson)*

- Lewis College of Business Lifetime Achievement Award

- Initiated by Joseph "Jack the Rapper" Gibson and donation from Jackie Wilson fans, a Prayer Bench placed at the Jackie Wilson Mausoleum at Westlawn Cemetery in Wayne, Michigan

- Motor City Music Awards' Lifetime Achievement Award

1999

- "Lonely Teardrops" and "(Your Love Keeps Lifting Me) Higher and Higher" inducted into the Grammy Hall of Fame

2002

- On Nov. 13, 2002, Jackie Wilson and Motown Records' house band, The Funk Brothers, were inducted into the Hollywood Rock Walk of Fame

2003 *(received posthumously by Brenda Wilson)*

- Detroit City Council Testimonial Resolution in honor of Jackie Wilson

- ·Wayne County Clerk Cathy Garrett's Office Resolution in honor of Jackie Wilson

2005 *(received posthumously by Brenda Wilson)*

- Inducted into the Internet Michigan Rock & Roll Legends Hall of Fame

2013 *(received posthumously by Brenda Wilson)*

- Inducted into the R&B Music Hall of Fame in Cleveland, Ohio

2015 *(received posthumously by Brenda Wilson)*

- Mayor Hubert Yopp and the City Council of Highland Park, Michigan, approved and renamed Cottage Grove Street to Jackie Wilson Lane.

- Re-inducted into the R&B Music Hall of Fame in Detroit, Michigan

2016 *(received posthumously by Brenda Wilson)*

- *State of Michigan gave special resolution tribute to Jackie Wilson on Aug. 20, 2016*

- The City of Detroit Mayor Michael Duggan sent a letter of congratulations and support to the Jackie Wilson Foundation, Inc.

- In Washington D.C., the National Museum of African American History and Culture opened September 24, 2016, and located at 1400 Constitution Ave. NW, in a ceremony led by U.S.

44th President Barack Obama. Jackie Wilson's name is located on a wall in the museum that commemorates iconic musical artists

2018

- Courtesy of the Hollywood Chamber of Commerce, it was announced on June 27, 2018 the list of artists who will be receiving stars on the Hollywood Walk of Fame in 2019: Robert De Niro leads the list that was unveiled. It is said that among the music stars who will be honored are the late, great, legendary Jackie Wilson, who will be honored posthumously, and collectively Linda Ronstadt, Dolly Parton and Emmylou Harris in recognition of their successful *Trio* series of albums

2019

- Brenda Wilson was given a float in the Annual St Clair Shores Memorial Day Parade representing "Mr. Entertainment" Jackie Wilson performers. On the float were singer Rob Carter performing Jackie Wilson songs, Thelma Stubbs Mitchell and the Stubbs Girl Group singing songs by Levi and Joe Stubbs; they were invited back for 2020 parade, however due to the COVID-19 Pandemic the parade was cancelled.

2020

The Star 2677 on the Hollywood Walk of Fame

On September 4, 2019, Jackie Wilson received the Star on the Hollywood Walk of Fame. This was a great day and it was long overdue for this Super Star.

Brenda and
Marshall Thompson
The Last Man Standing
The Original Chi Lites

The Hollywood Group

My family and friends were all in attendance with me from Detroit and other states. Also Jackie's granddaughter Erika Johnson, Thelma Stubbs Mitchell, Levi Stubbs' sister, and Jackie's cousin, friend of the family Theresa Rose Randleson, Dr Roman Franklin (Dr. Doo Wop), Paul and Theresa Lowe, Tyrone Williamson, Mahonale and Irene Air Bed & Breakfast host.

A special thanks to Gary Hunter, the photographer, who met us in Hollywood. I also received the authentic replica of the Hollywood Star. Speakers for the ceremony were Mary Wilson, Smokey Robinson, Marshall Thompson and Berry Gordy, as well as many other family members, friends and fans.

The Detroit Youth Choir was in Hollywood for American Idol at that time … Mr. Anthony White, Director of the DYC, was in attendance at the Hollywood Walk of Fame. He asked me if I could come over to the Lowes Hotel were the choir was staying and that the choir was going to do a special presentation for me. Of course, I said yes.

So, at 2:00 p.m., me and our group went over to the Lowes Hotel where the Detroit Youth Choir all came together.

They sung their special rendition of "Higher and Higher." It was awesome. Those kids did a wonderful job. Everyone was in tears after they finished singing to me. They all wanted their own hug and I hugged each and every one of them. It was a special thank you from me and my father.

The love they shared with me and the love for my father Jackie Wilson was a historical moment that their generation will always remember that day and time as the tribute they sang for Jackie Wilson and me, his daughter, Brenda Wilson.

The Detroit Youth Choir won second place on "American Idol." Although they won second place, they will always be first place winners to me and in my heart. The choir is great and they are doing great things in the music industry.

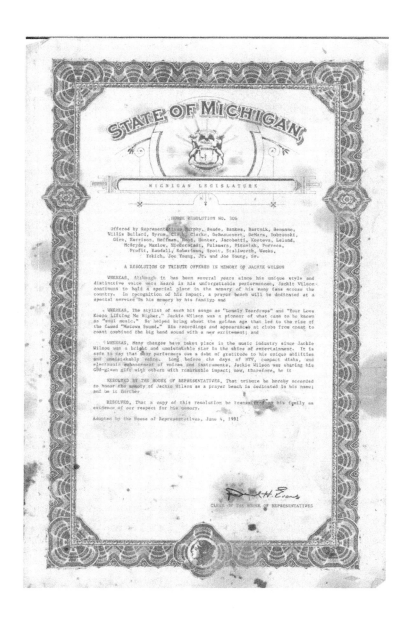

STATE OF MICHIGAN

MICHIGAN LEGISLATURE

HOUSE RESOLUTION NO. 306

Offered by Representatives Murphy, Bende, Bankes, Bartnik, Bennane,
Willis Bullard, Byrum, Clark, Clarke, DeBeaussert, DeMars, Dobronski,
Gire, Harrison, Hoffman, Hood, Hunter, Jacobetti, Kosteva, Leland,
McBryde, Maxlow, Niederstadt, Palsawara, Pitoniak, Porreca,
Profit, Randall, Robertson, Scott, Stallworth, Weeks,
Yokich, Joe Young, Jr. and Joe Young, Sr.

A RESOLUTION OF TRIBUTE OFFERED IN MEMORY OF JACKIE WILSON

WHEREAS, Although it has been several years since his unique style and
distinctive voice were heard in his unforgettable performances, Jackie Wilson
continues to hold a special place in the memory of his many fans across the
country. In recognition of his impact, a prayer bench will be dedicated at a
special service in his memory by his family; and

WHEREAS, The stylist of such hit songs as "Lonely Teardrops" and "Your Love
Keeps Lifting Me Higher," Jackie Wilson was a pioneer of what came to be known
as "soul music." He helped bring about the golden age that led to the rise of
the famed "Motown Sound." His recordings and appearances at clubs from coast to
coast combined the big band sound with a new excitement; and

WHEREAS, Many changes have taken place in the music industry since Jackie
Wilson was a bright and unmistakable star in the skies of entertainment. It is
safe to say that many performers owe a debt of gratitude to his unique abilities
and unmistakable voice. Long before the days of MTV, compact disks, and
electronic enhancement of voices and instruments, Jackie Wilson was sharing his
God-given gift with others with remarkable impact; now, therefore, be it

RESOLVED BY THE HOUSE OF REPRESENTATIVES, That tribute be hereby accorded
to honor the memory of Jackie Wilson as a prayer bench is dedicated in his name;
and be it further

RESOLVED, That a copy of this resolution be transmitted to his family as
evidence of our respect for his memory.

Adopted by the House of Representatives, June 4, 1991

CLERK OF THE HOUSE OF REPRESENTATIVES

125

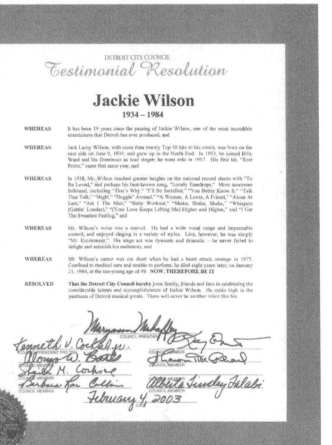

DETROIT CITY COUNCIL
Testimonial Resolution

Jackie Wilson
1934 – 1984

WHEREAS   It has been 19 years since the passing of Jackie Wilson, one of the most incredible entertainers that Detroit has ever produced, and

WHEREAS   Jack Leroy Wilson, with more than twenty Top 40 hits to his credit, was born on the east side on June 9, 1934, and grew up in the North End. In 1953, he joined Billy Ward and his Dominoes as lead singer; he went solo in 1957. His first hit, "Reet Petite," came that same year, and

WHEREAS   In 1958, Mr. Wilson reached greater heights on the national record charts with "To Be Loved," and perhaps his best-known song, "Lonely Teardrops." More successes followed, including "That's Why," "I'll Be Satisfied," "You Better Know It," "Talk That Talk," "Night," "Doggin' Around," "A Woman, A Lover, A Friend," "Alone At Last," "Am I The Man," "Baby Workout," "Shake, Shake, Shake," "Whispers (Gettin' Louder)," "(Your Love Keeps Lifting Me) Higher and Higher," and "I Get The Sweetest Feeling," and

WHEREAS   Mr. Wilson's voice was a marvel. He had a wide vocal range and impeccable control, and enjoyed singing in a variety of styles. Live, however, he was simply "Mr. Excitement." His stage act was dynamic and dramatic – he never failed to delight and astonish his audiences, and

WHEREAS   Mr. Wilson's career was cut short when he had a heart attack onstage in 1975. Confined to medical care and unable to perform, he died eight years later, on January 21, 1984, at the too-young age of 49. NOW, THEREFORE BE IT

RESOLVED   That the Detroit City Council hereby joins family, friends and fans in celebrating the considerable talents and accomplishments of Jackie Wilson. He ranks high in the pantheon of Detroit musical greats. There will never be another voice like his.

February 4, 2003

STATE OF MICHIGAN

SPECIAL TRIBUTE

JACKIE WILSON

"Courage is the most important of all virtues, because without it we can't practice any other virtue with consistency." ~Maya Angelou

LET IT BE KNOWN, That, I and my colleagues join in the street naming celebration of one of our beloved and legendary singer and entertainer, Mr. Jackie Wilson. Cottage Grove Street in the City of Highland Park, Michigan is now known as Jackie Wilson Lane.

Jackie Leroy Wilson was born on June 9, 1934 to Jackie and Eliza Wilson on the east side of Detroit, Michigan.

He was educated in the Detroit Public School system and at an early age, he joined Russell Street Baptist Church where he was baptized.

After a brief period of time as an amateur boxer, Jackie turned to music. Before there was "Motown," Mr. Wilson collaborated with Berry Gordy Jr. who produced six hits. At the age of fifteen, Jackie Wilson was a part of the great tradition of Black Entertainment that played dates and clubs in the Paradise Theater in Detroit, Michigan. He gave us iconic songs like *"Lonely Teardrops," "Your Love Keeps Lifting Me"* and *"To Be Loved."*

But it was Jackie's electrifying performances, soulful presence and smooth moves that his audiences loved and others were influenced by. Such as: Elvis Presley, James Brown and Michael Jackson, just to name a few. He sold over six million copies of his recordings and was loved by his fans and respected by his peers. Jackie Wilson was truly one of the greatest entertainers to come out of Detroit.

In 1975, Mr. Wilson suffered a heart attack while in Cherry Hill, New Jersey and was never able to perform again. After a long illness, Jackie passed away January 21, 1984. He left on this earth to remember him sweetly, his children: Anthony Wilson, Brenda Wilson, Foley Jay Wilson, John Dominique Wilson, Li-nie Wilson, Sabrina Bynum Wilson and a host of friends, fans and admirers.

IN SPECIAL TRIBUTE, Therefore, this document is signed and sealed in memory, honor and celebration of the icon singer and entertainer, Jackie Wilson. With family, friends and many fans, we salute the man, his memory and congratulate his proud family who can ride down a street in Highland Park, Michigan named Jackie Wilson Lane.

The Honorable Coleman A. Young, II, State Senator
The First District

The Ninety-Eighth Legislature
At Lansing
August 20, 2016

The City of Detroit

Office of the Mayor

A Tribute to

Jackie Wilson

With the moniker "Mr. Excitement," Jack Leroy "Jackie" Wilson, Jr was a master showman and one of the most influential artists of his generation. A Rock and Roll Hall of Fame and a Grammy Hall of Fame inductee, Jackie Wilson is one of the greatest artists of all time.

Born in Detroit, Jackie Wilson turned to music after a brief period of time as an amateur boxer. Before there was Motown, Jackie collaborated with Berry Gordy, Jr., to produce six hits. And as much a lyricist as he was a vocalist, Jackie Wilson gave us iconic songs like "Lonely Teardrops," "(Your Love Keeps Lifting Me) Higher and Higher," and "To Be Loved." Who wouldn't come home to Jackie Wilson crooning, "just say you will... say you will."

But it was Jackie's electrifying performances that influenced the likes of Elvis Presley, Michael Jackson and James Brown. Jackie's effort to control his performances were evident; he led an era when being classy was as valued as being talented. But Jackie's gospel roots and soulful presence always resonated and moved his audience; once ending a television performance of "To Be Loved" with a run more likely to be heard by folks in church pews on Sunday morning, rather than during primetime on Sunday nights.

And during Jackie's first television appearance on The Ed Sullivan Show, Sullivan referred to Jackie as "being beloved by his own people," but Jackie didn't sell over 6 million copies being beloved by his "own" people. Jackie Wilson was beloved by all. Jackie Wilson was charismatic, versatile and "exquisitely soulful." He's one of the greatest to come out of Detroit and we're glad he found music and hung up his boxing gloves.

Today, on behalf of the City of Detroit, I join Jackie Wilson's family, friends and many fans, as well as the City of Highland Park, in recognizing that henceforth Cottage Grove Street will be known as Jackie Wilson Lane. And we thank Jackie Wilson for the music that lifts us higher and higher.

MAYOR, CITY OF DETROIT

August 20, 2016

DATE

CHAPTER TWELVE

The Legacy Continues ...

Although the Bible tells us to let our works praise us in the gate (Proverbs 31:31), for the purpose of this publication, I will share with you some of my personal accomplishments and milestones. Thereby, letting you know that the legacy continues ...

I am the daughter of the late Jackie Wilson, an international recording legend. For over 30 years, I have been an entrepreneur with experience in the music industry as a producer of live shows, vocalist and talent scouting. I am the Founder and CEO of the Jackie Wilson Foundation, Inc., a non-profit organization, founder of God In Me (G.I.M.) Production Company, and owner of OoWee Homemade Ice Cream.

In 1990, when I started promoting and producing the "Apollo Live of Michigan," I didn't know the full history of my father's entertainment beginning, such as how he started performing at the amateur talent shows around Detroit. This idea was given to me one day as I was walking through the Warehouse Club in Detroit for a meeting. That's when the Holy Spirit dropped the idea in my spirit, and I went full steam ahead to bring the show into existence for six months.

Starting in June 1990, and every fourth Wednesday of the month after that, at the Warehouse Club, was the birth of the "Hottest Show in the State of Michigan." There were over 800 people in the audience and a line out the door of people trying to get in to see singers, dancers, comedians, and musicians showcase their great talent in the show. This show moved from the Warehouse Club to the famous Latin Quarters on East Grand Blvd in Detroit because the Warehouse couldn't hold all the people.

The attendance rose to over 1500 people at each show. It continued to be held every month on the fourth Wednesday.

Brenda created the "Offsprings of Legends" showcase, "Groupin It Up," and "Offsprings of Legends" TV Show, under the direction of the Wilson Entertainment Group, Inc. Entities have been created to give a platform and opportunities for youth and young adults to showcase their raw talent in the entertainment and music industry in front of live audiences. I am continuing even now: creating, producing, directing, and promoting.

My works include Jackie Wilson Tributes and serving as a celebrity judge for talent showcases. I have worked with many well-known celebrities, including Hollywood actor/producer Robert Townsend, Dick Clark, the Reverend Jesse Jackson, Montel Williams, *Good Times* actress Bernadette Stanis, gospel recording artists the Clark Sisters, Take Six, Bishop Rance Allen, Motown Records' legendary group the Contours, the Stubbs Girls, music legend James Brown and Little Richard, The Falcons, David Washington of the TV One series *Unsung*, the legendary group the Fantastic Four, Rob Carter, Mary Wilson of the Supremes, Martha Reeves and the Vandellas, Phase Five and producer David Usher, and more.

Dick Clark and Brenda

I have interviewed and hosted the legendary girls group "Xscape" and "Offsprings of Legends," such as Ray Charles, Sam Cooke, Willie Dixon, David Ruffin, Enchantment, the rap group Detroit's Most Wanted Rappers, Marvin Gaye, Berry Gordy, Lou Rawls, Freddy Pride, guitarist Billy Davis, and many, many more.

The Jackie Wilson Foundation sees the need to establish the Jackie Wilson Performing Arts Theatre to continue offering affordable opportunity for individuals in different communities to showcase their talents. My history over the past 30 years of successful production of talent showcases, plays and concerts for live audiences paved the way for this Jackie Wilson Performing Arts Theatre.

In 1994, while in California on vacation, I stayed in Santa Monica. It was there that I had the opportunity to meet and visit many influential people. One person I really wanted to meet was Dick Clark because of the relationship he had with my father. I had scheduled an appointment to meet with him at his office. Mr. Clark was a very nice and welcoming person. He showed me around his offices and Universal Studios. After we toured, we sat down and talked. He also shared interesting stories about my father. He told me if I were to redo any of my father's music, "Not to change a thing."

He shared that Sony Music wanted to do a movie about Jackie's life, that it was being negotiated, and he would let me know the outcome. He said, "I'll call you."

Well, he did call me a few weeks later and said, "Brenda, it is not going to happen."

"Why not? I asked, disappointedly.

Clark answered, "The Wilson family didn't want it to happen." "Why?" I asked. "That doesn't make sense."

"I don't know, but it's not going to happen." "OK, thanks for letting me know."

The conversation closed with Clark telling me I could call him anytime. And I did. Dick Clark and I kept in contact for a good while. He passed away April 18, 2012. To me Dick Clark always looked the same.

Brenda's Accomplishments &
Milestones, 1990-2020

1990

- Producer and promoter of the "Apollo Live of Michigan" Talent Show for Detroit and Ann Arbor, Michigan.

  The event was the biggest monthly family talent showcase in Michigan and was held at the Latin Quarter in Detroit on the fourth Wednesday of each month.

  The shows featured youth and young adult performers from the communities, including singers, dancers, rappers, comedians, musicians, celebrity judges and special guest performances. It was hosted by radio personalities from stations of all formats, including R&B, jazz, etc.

- The Gospel Apolloship held on the second Sunday of each month

1991

- Brenda Winner of three Emmys for songwriting, audio recording, and videography (co-song writer with Kimberly Jackson); the song, "We Need a City," for the City for Youth project that won 10 Emmys for PBS Channel 56, Brenda Co-Writer of Theme Song.

- Member of Grammy Awards Committee and attended the Grammys in New York the same year that M. C. Hammer won his first Grammy for Best Song, Best Music Film and Best Rap Solo Performance, "U Can't Touch This."

- Producer of theme song, choir and video for the City for Youth project for PBS Channel 56. Co-writer of theme song, "We Need a City" and producer of the diverse, 70-member City for Youth Choir. Recorded the song and produced a video. This project was syndicated across the country for five days, and the theme, "We Need a City," was played in all promotional materials on all media outlets. The City for Youth project won Emmys.

1992

- Producer of the NAACP Detroit Choir for a competition performance in the state of Michigan
- Produced program for Joseph "Jack the Rapper" Gibson, the Jackie Wilson Prayer Bench Ceremony held at Westlawn Cemetery in Wayne, Michigan

- Promoter and host of the play "The Devil Made Me Do It" at the Masonic Temple in Detroit

1993

- Producer of choir of local talent to perform for the Michigan Annual Thanksgiving Day Parade

- Producer of the "Hair War Competition" for *Beauty Shop 3* at the Music Hall in Downtown Detroit.

1994

- Producer and promoter of "Montel Williams Live," three days of TV broadcasts from the former State Theatre in Downtown Detroit. Segment entitled "The Motown Review," featured Detroit's finest raw talent performing impersonations of Stevie Wonder, the Marvelettes, the Contours, the Temptations and Mary Wells. The showcase was a major success.

2001

- Graduate of Word of Faith International Christian Center Laymen's Ministry School

2003

- Spokesperson for the family: The play, *My Heart Is*

Crying, Crying, premiered at the Music Hall in Downtown Detroit.

Jackie Taylor, director of the Black Ensemble Theater in Chicago, contacted Brenda Wilson about bringing Jackie Wilson's story to the stage. She contacted the Wilson Family.

The Wilson family received a special tribute from the Michigan State Representative Artina Tinsley Hardman, a resolution from Wayne County Clerk Cathy Garrett and a resolution from the office of Detroit City Councilwoman Kay Everett, honoring Jackie Wilson in support of the play.

The state presented its written tribute on stage to Jackie's children Thor, Foley Jay, Lanai and Brenda, who served as the family spokesperson and made sure that each of her siblings received a copy.

The rest of the Wilson family was in the audience. Received Posthumously by Brenda Wilson the Detroit City Council Testimonial Resolution

2004

- Route Supervisor for the John Kerry Campaign for President

- G.I.M. Production Company, with our new artist

Erika who produced and wrote the song entitled, "America Coming Together" and performed for Rev. Jesse Jackson at the Northwest Activities Center in Detroit, Michigan

2009

- Brenda Wilson started "Friday Night Jams with Brenda Wilson and Friends" at the Music Hall Jazz Cafe with singers' and rappers' nights.

2011

- Successful producer and promoter of "Brenda Wilson and Friends" at the Music Hall Jazz Cafe in Downtown Detroit. A showcase of local talent singers of all genres of music and local rappers.

2015

- Presenter for the Detroit Music Awards at the Fillmore Detroit

- Presenter for the Detroit Black Music Awards at the Bert's Warehouse Theatre Detroit's Eastern Market district

- Master of Ceremonies for the R&B Music Hall of Fame, held at the Charles H. Wright Museum of

African American History in Detroit

- Received posthumously second Induction Award from the R & B Music Hall of Fame for Jackie Wilson.

- Successfully created, produced, and promoted the "Offspring of Legends" live stage production of "Groupin It Up," a showcase for "Offspring of Legends," working with the offspring of the legendary Ray Charles and Sam Cooke with special guest performances. The showcase featured "Groupin It Up" with local talent from all over Michigan of all ages in competition.

- Successfully initiated and spearheaded the effort to successfully obtain all votes from the Highland Park City Council to rename Cottage Grove Street "Jackie Wilson Lane," where he once lived in Highland Park, Michigan.

- Founded the Jackie Wilson Foundation, Inc. 501(c)3

- Member of the Writers Guild of America East, Inc.

- Honored for Outstanding Leadership and

Commitment by The National Association of Professional Women.

2016

- Owner of the Jackie Wilson Trademark, a multimedia entertainment services, recording, music, video, film, production and post-production (2016-2018)

- Jackie Wilson Street Naming Celebration. Obtained sponsorship from the UAW Ford and Jackie Wilson Foundation, Inc., for the Jackie Wilson Street Naming Celebration on Aug. 20, 2016, with coverage by national and international social and TV media.

It was held at the WHPR TV Studio located on Victor Street in Highland Park with over 500 in attendance. The celebration featured special guest performances from worldwide recording artists and Grammy winners Bishop Rance Allen, the Contours, the Stubbs Girls, Rob Carter and a tribute to Jackie Wilson from his grandson, rapper Reggie "Motsi Ski" Abrams.

The keynote speaker was Mary Wilson of the Supreme, and there were presentations and acknowledgements from Michigan federal and state representatives, Mayor Hubert Yopp of Highland Park, the Highland Park City Council, Detroit Mayor Michael Duggan, the Detroit City Council and memories shared by a host of family and friends.

2017

- Presenter for the Detroit Black Music Awards at the Charles H. Wright Museum of African American History in Detroit

- Graduate of Fisherman Evangelistic Ministries Inc.

- Represented the late Jackie Wilson for the presentation of his name for a historical marker at United Sound Systems Recording Studios in Detroit

- Hosted live TV recording of the Bravo reality series Xscape Still Kickin' It at United Sound Systems Recording Studios in Detroit

- Interviewed on "American Black Journal" for Father's Day show

- Recorded at historic United Sound Systems Recording Studios the opening and closing line for a documentary

- Performed at Hug Detroit Day Backpack & School Supplies Donation event

- Performed in a tribute to the Jackie Wilson Story through songs at the Comprehensive Services for the Developmentally Disabled in New Haven, Michigan, with legendary vocalist Venus Ford, Sandy Bomar, Lisa Herring and Rock & Roll Hall of Fame guitarist Billy Davis.

2018

- Traveled to Baden-Baden, Germany with Shirley King for the show to be recorded "I Bare a Famous Name"

- A producer for the Motown Amplified Talent Search

- Maker and Owner of OoWee Homemade Ice Cream was sold in the famous Bert's Warehouse in Detroit

2019

- Brenda Wilson a producer and promoter of the Motown Amplify Showcase at the Garden Theater, located in Detroit, featuring upcoming talented youth and young adults from all communities over the State of Michigan

- Committee Member for the R&B Music Hall of Fame and a Presenter of the Jackie Wilson Icon Award

- Co-Owner of Bre-Th Production and Management Company

- Recipient of the "Hug Detroit" Lifetime Achievement Award

- A producer for the Motown Amplified Talent Search

- Contributed artists The Stubb's Girls and artist Kamaria to perform on the Ball Room Express TV Show

- Vocalist in original song regarding women affected by Domestic Violence, "Breaking the Silence," written by Chelly K

- Featured upcoming artist Kamaria on the River Days 3 Event in downtown Detroit

- Robin Terry, president of Motown, received Detroit "thank you" award presented to her by Brenda Wilson and Beth Griffith Manley for all Motown support to our communities for our youth

- Bre-Th Production Company showcased our artist Kamaria on "The Detroit Rib N Soul Fest" in Detroit

2020

- A special thanks to the late State Representative Isaac Robinson for presenting all the "Offsprings of Legends" a resolution from The State of Michigan for their showcase on February 23, 2020 at the Northwest Activities Center

- Producer of the Next Level Showcase on February 23 held at the Northwestern Activities Center, featuring "Offsprings of Legends" such as Bendito King son of Ben E, King, "Stand by Me," Brenda Taylor Ricci, daughter of Eddie Taylor, "Baby What You Want Me To Do," Rose Reed, daughter of Jimmy Reed, "Bright Lights Big City, Joseph Morganfield, son of Muddie Waters, "You got that MOJO Working," Brenda Wilson, daughter of Jackie Wilson, "To Be Loved," Jenitia Que Hodges, daughter of Jody Thomas. "It's You That I Need," The Stubbs group nieces, Sheila Taylor, Pam Fuller, Robin Pierce and Rhoda Robinson of Levi and Joe Stubbs, and Thelma Stubbs Mitchell, sister of Levi and Joe Stubbs. The upcoming talent featured was Mighty Mike, Versatile, Larmar Anthem and Venus Ford.

- Special Guest Performers: Joe "Pep" Harris and

Undisputed Truth, Legendary Billy Davis, Guitarist, Rob Carter, The Young Men for Christ, Gospel group and John Hall.

- A special thanks to the late State Representative Isaac Robinson for presenting Rodger Penzabene, Jr. with a Resolution from the State of Michigan and recognizing his father for his contribution with Motown as a producer and songwriter.

- Sherry Gay–Dagnogo, M.Ed.. Representative of The Eighth District, Chair of The Detroit Caucus of Michigan's 100th Legislative celebrates and recognizes in a special tribute to honor and commend Brenda Wilson for her impressive career. May she know of our admiration and warmest wishes for continued success.

- Sherry Gay–Dagnogo also gave special recognition awards to all the "Offsprings of Legends" in attendance during the showcase on February 23, 2020 at the Northwest Activities Center.

- Brenda received the Highest Recognition Award from the late State Representative Isaac Robinson, "The Great Seal of the State of Michigan/Music Industry Legend. We honor the state representative who passed in March 2020 from COVID-19

- Brenda was to be inducted into the R & B Music Hall of Fame, however, because of COVID-19, it is being rescheduled for 2021.

VOLUNTEER SERVICES

- I support and volunteer for organizations throughout the United States, serving as Master of Ceremonies, Celebrity Host and Judge, and also as a vocalist-entertainer.

Awards

- "The Great Seal of the State of Michigan" Award

- Resolutions from: Former U.S. Congressman John Conyers (Michigan),

- Michigan State Representative—Coleman A. Young, Jr.,

- Mayor of City of Detroit (Michigan)—Michael Duggan

- The Detroit City Council Resolution

- Wayne County (Michigan) Commission

- Brenda has received numerous awards from many different diverse Communities and Organizations

THE NATIONAL ACADEMY OF TELEVISION ARTS & SCIENCES
MICHIGAN CHAPTER

For a Significant Contribution to the EMMY® Award for Excellence
Given to

Brenda Wilson
(Songwriter)

For

Audio Recording and Video
'We Need a City"

WTVS
June 1, 1991

STATE OF MICHIGAN

SPECIAL TRIBUTE

To

BRENDA WILSON

Let It Be Known, it is with great pleasure that I recognize Brenda Wilson for continuing the great legacy of community development and public service.

Most Detroiter's remember the late great Jackie Wilson as "Mr. Excitement" an outstanding performer who recorded the legendary hits Lonely Teardrops; To Be Loved, Your Love Is Lifting Me Higher and Higher. He was an inspiration to many musicians including Chuck Berry, Little Richard, Elvis Presley and Michael Jackson. Brenda Wilson who is also a vocalist and incredibly talented, has carried the family tradition in her own right.

Since 1990, Brenda Wilson, has been an entrepreneur, producer, and executive director of the entertainment company God In Me (G.I.M.) Production, Co. and OOWee! Homemade Ice Cream, LLC.

She also performed vocally at many corporate events, wedding, private parties, churches and she has been a celebrity judge for many local talent showcases.

Brenda has been involved as the producer of the successful Apollo Live of Michigan Talent Showcase, Gospel ApolloShip Talent Search, Jackie Wilson Tribute, TV-56 City for Youth choir project including the video and theme song and the NAACP Gospel Choir. Her venues in the metropolitan Detroit area included the West Grand Boulevard "Twenty Grand", the Rackham Building Auditorium, The Community Auditorium on Wayne State University Campus, and Historic King Solomon Baptist Church.

Brenda believes in giving back to the community. She is involved in volunteering, fund-raising activities, concerts and gospel music productions. The educational arm of her organization provides workshops and seminars on self-improvement and motivational skills, as well as addressing topics relevant to the entertainment industry.

IN SPECIAL TRIBUTE, therefore, this document is dedicated to honor Brenda Wilson for continuing the legacy of greatness, and community and public service.

Fred Durhal, III, State Representative
Assistant Democratic Leader
The Fifth District

The Ninety-Eighth Legislature
At Lansing
Friday, February 28, 2015

Certificate of Special Congressional Recognition

Presented to

Brenda Wilson

In honor of

**YOUR SIGNIFICANT CONTRIBUTIONS TO
THE MUSIC INDUSTRY**

*In Detroit, Michigan
Presented on Saturday, the 28th Day of February, 2015*

HONORABLE JOHN CONYERS, JR.
Member of Congress
13th District of Michigan

COUNTY OF WAYNE
MICHIGAN

Resolution

HONORING
MS. BRENDA WILSON
Groupin It Up

WHEREAS, BRENDA WILSON is an entrepreneur, producer, and the executive director of the entertainment company God In Me (G.I.M.) Productions and OOWee! Homemade Ice Cream, LLC since 1990.

WHEREAS, BRENDA WILSON is an incredibly talented vocalist who has performed at many corporate events, weddings, private parties and churches. She has also served as a celebrity judge for many local talent showcases.

WHEREAS, BRENDA WILSON, was the producer of the extremely successful Apollo Live of Michigan Talent Showcase, as well as, The Gospel Apollo Ship Talent Search, Jackie Wilson Tribute, and TV-56 City of Youth choir project which included the video and theme song for the NAACP Gospel Choir. Her incredible talent has taken her to various venues in the City of Detroit ranging from The "Twenty Grand" (West Grand Blvd), Wayne State University Campus and the Historic King Solomon Baptist Church.

WHEREAS, BRENDA WILSON, Special Event Coordinator skills has positioned her to achieve many accomplishments producing a multitude of trips, choirs, schools, and showcasing various events.

WHEREAS, BRENDA WILSON, believes in giving back to the community; she is involved in volunteering, overseeing fund-raising activities, hosting concerts and gospel music productions.

WHEREAS, BRENDA WILSON, provides workshops and seminars on self-improvement and motivational skills, as well as addressing topics relevant to the entertainment industry. **THEREFORE LET IT BE**

RESOLVED, I, Cathy M. Garrett, Wayne County Clerk, join with the host of family and friends in saluting and commending **MS. BRENDA WILSON**, on this 28th day of February, 2015. As I present this resolution in recognition of your dedicated and service to our community, let it be a lasting record of respect and appreciation.

Cathy M. Garrett
WAYNE COUNTY CLERK

153

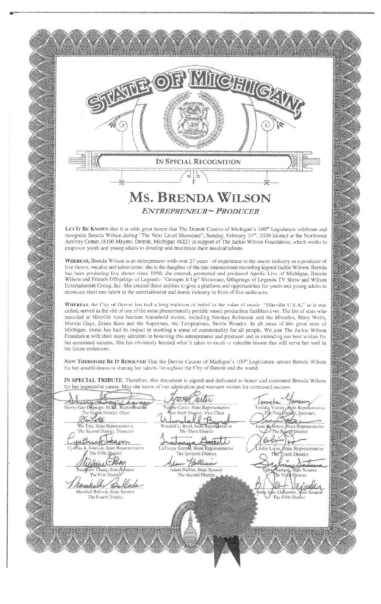

STATE OF MICHIGAN

IN SPECIAL RECOGNITION

MS. BRENDA WILSON
ENTREPRENEUR ~ PRODUCER

LET IT BE KNOWN that it is with great honor that The Detroit Caucus of Michigan's 100th Legislature celebrate and recognize Brenda Wilson during "The Next Level Showcase", Sunday, February 23rd, 2020 located at the Northwest Activity Center, 18100 Meyers, Detroit, Michigan 48221 in support of The Jackie Wilson Foundation; which works to empower youth and young adults to develop and maximize their musical talents.

WHEREAS, Brenda Wilson is an entrepreneur with over 27 years' of experience in the music industry as a producer of live shows, vocalist and talent scout; she is the daughter of the late international recording legend Jackie Wilson. Brenda has been producing live shows since 1990, she created, promoted and produced Apollo Live of Michigan, Brenda Wilson and Friends Offsprings of Legends- "Groupin It Up" Showcase, Offsprings of Legends TV Show and Wilson Entertainment Group, Inc. She created these entities to give a platform and opportunities for youth and young adults to showcase their raw talent in the entertainment and music industry in front of live audiences.

WHEREAS, the City of Detroit has had a long tradition of belief in the value of music "Hitsville U.S.A." as it was called, served as the site of one of the most phenomenally prolific music production facilities ever. The list of stars who recorded at Hitsville have become household names, including Smokey Robinson and the Miracles, Mary Wells, Marvin Gaye, Diana Ross and the Supremes, the Temptations, Stevie Wonder. In all areas of this great state of Michigan, music has had its impact in marking a sense of commonality for all people. We join The Jackie Wilson Foundation with their many admirers in honoring this entrepreneur and producer and in extending our best wishes for her continued success. She has obviously learned what it takes to excel--a valuable lesson that will serve her well in his future endeavors.

NOW THEREFORE BE IT RESOLVED That the Detroit Caucus of Michigan's 100th Legislature salutes Brenda Wilson for her unselfishness in sharing her talents throughout the City of Detroit and the world.

IN SPECIAL TRIBUTE, Therefore, this document is signed and dedicated to honor and commend Brenda Wilson for her impressive career. May she know of our admiration and warmest wishes for continued success.

Sherry Gay-Dagnogo, M. Ed., Representative
The Eighth District, Chair

Tyrone Carter, State Representative
The Sixth District, Vice Chair

Tenisha Yancey, State Representative
The First District, Secretary

Joe Tate, State Representative
The Second District, Treasurer

Wendall L. Byrd, State Representative
The Third District

Isaac Robinson, State Representative
The Fourth District

Cynthia A. Johnson, State Representative
The Fifth District

LaTanya Garrett, State Representative
The Seventh District

Leslie Love, State Representative
The Tenth District

Stephanie Chang, State Senator
The First District

Adam Hollier, State Senator
The Second District

Sylvia Santana, State Senator
The Third District

Marshall Bullock, State Senator
The Fourth District

Betty Jean Alexander, State Senator
The Fifth District

CERTIFICATE OF
RECOGNITION

On behalf of its citizens, I, the Mayor of the City of Detroit,
proudly honor

Ms. Brenda Wilson

(Offspring of the late Jackie Wilson)
And the Jackie Wilson Foundation, Inc.
On *"the Next Level"* Showcase Fundraiser
May your accomplishments serve as an inspiration to others!

Mayor

February 23, 2020
Date

CITY OF
DETROIT

Rep. Isaac
Robinson
2-20-2?

Brenda Wilson
The Great Seal of the State of Michigan

This symbol of sovereignty was adopted in 1911 by the Michigan legislature from a design drawn by Michigan's territorial governor, Lewis Cass, in 1835. The Latin phrases on the seal, translated, say: "E Pluribus Unum," one out of many; "Tuebor," I will protect; and "Si quaeris peninsulam amoenam, circumspice," if you seek a pleasant peninsula, look about you. The coat of arms forms the center of the seal and is encircled by the words, "The Great Seal of the State of Michigan."

Music Industry Legend

DID YOU KNOW?

DID YOU KNOW?

Jackie's favorite song to sing growing up was "Danny Boy."

DID YOU KNOW?

"Reet Petite (The Finest Girl You Ever Wanna Meet)" peaked at #62 on the Billboard Hot 100 in September 1957 and reached # 6 on the UK singles chart.

DID YOU KNOW?

In 1986, two years after Jackie's death, the song "Reet Petite" was re—released in 1986 as Reet Petite (The Sweetest Girl in Town), and it became so popular that by December 1986 it became #1 in the UK for four weeks, selling over 700,000 copies. This was 29 years after its first chart debut.

DID YOU KNOW?

"(Your Love Keeps Lifting Me) Higher and Higher"
(a #1 R&B and #6 pop hit on the Billboard charts)
was recorded on July 6, 1967, at Columbia Studios
and produced by Carl Davis during a session
arranged by Sonny Sander, featuring James
Jamerson on bass, Richard "Pistol" Allen on drums,
Robert White on guitar and Johnny Griffith on
keyboard.

These were all members of Motown Records' house
band, The Funk Brothers. According to Carl Davis,
they would load up their van in Detroit on the
weekends and go to Chicago. "I would pay 'em
double scale, and I'd pay them in cash,"he recalled.

DID YOU KNOW?

Two of Motown's house session singers the Andantes,
Jackie Hicks and Marlene Barrow, along with Pat
Lewis performed on the session for "Higher and
Higher."

DID YOU KNOW?

Billy Davis said, "Lonely Teardrops" was originally
written as a blues ballad, and it was tossed in the

garbage. It was taken out, and Nat Tarnopol gave it to famous composer and orchestra director Dick Jacobs to rearrange.

DID YOU KNOW?

There was a wonderful clip captured on Nov. 3, 1964 from the dance show "Talent Party" on WHBQ TV in Memphis, Tennessee.

It does not appear to be a broadcast performance for Jackie Wilson and Sam Cooke, but the camera and microphone were on, according to a documentary on Cooke. He had no clue that Jackie was there, and he was totally caught by surprise when he saw him. But they were good friends and had a lot of fun doing Cooke's song, "Everybody Loves to Cha Cha Cha," as a duet.

DID YOU KNOW?

Jackie was also an animal lover. He owned a brown Chihuahua named Poochie who traveled with him. August Sims, his valet, would be responsible for getting Poochie's food and taking care of the dog while Jackie was on stage.

He was also a very contemplative and deep thinker and his favorite drink was Smirnoff vodka.

DID YOU KNOW?

Mario Lanza, a famous Italian opera star, was Jackie's idol. He liked him so much that he developed his own opera style because Jackie couldn't read the music lead sheets.

DID YOU KNOW?

"To Be Loved," written by Berry Gordy, is my favorite song, and I sing it all the time in my shows.

DID YOU KNOW?

When Dick Clark found out that Jackie was broke, he committed to paying his medical bills for eight years until the day Jackie died.

DID YOU KNOW?

Henry Washington, brother of David Washington (commentator on TV One's "Unsung"), was the promo man for Brunswick Records from June 1973 to June 1974 for Jackie.

<u>DID YOU KNOW?</u>

Jackie had six consecutive hit singles between 1958 and 1959, which made him a superstar.

<u>DID YOU KNOW?</u>

There were two sides to records, the A-side and the B-side.

The A-side featured the recording that the producer or record company wanted to promote and receive radio airplay, hopefully to become a hit. The B-side (or flip side) would sometimes become a hit in its own right.

<u>DID YOU KNOW?</u>

The song "Nights" was an A-side, the B-side was "Doggin' Around," and both were big hits.

<u>DID YOU KNOW?</u>

Jackie Wilson, Sam Cooke and Ray Charles were great friends. Brenda Wilson, executive producer and promoter, created the show "Offsprings of Legends" and featured the daughters of Sam Cooke, Ray Charles, and herself as judges for a community talent show — with great success.

DID YOU KNOW?

Jackie Wilson and Sam Cooke received the same honor in their hometowns. Cooke had a street named after him in June 2011 called "Sam Cooke Way," on 36th Street and Cottage Grove in Chicago, Illinois. Jackie had one named after him in August 2016 called "Jackie Wilson Lane" on Cottage Grove Street and Woodward Avenue in Highland Park, Michigan.

DID YOU KNOW?

That Brunswick Records still owed him unpaid royalties.

DID YOU KNOW?

"Lonely Teardrops" was a million-seller, and Dick Clark had a "Lonely Teardrops" gold record in his office.

DID YOU KNOW?

Jackie Wilson's 1958 hit, "To Be Loved," co-written by Motown Records founder, Berry Gordy, was the title of the mogul's autobiography published in 1995.

DID YOU KNOW?

"I'll Be Satisfied" reached #6 on Billboard's R&B chart and #20 on the Hot 100 in 1959 and was covered by a wide variety of artists, including blues legend Ruth Brown, "Soul Queen of New Orleans" Irma Thomas and country singer Don Adams.

DID YOU KNOW?

Rolling Stone magazine placed Jackie Wilson at #26 on its list of 100 Greatest Singers of All Time, right between "King of Pop" Michael Jackson at #25 and country legend Hank Williams at #27.

DID YOU KNOW?

Cornelius Gunther, a member of the Coasters group that was to perform on the Dick Clark show on the night Jackie Wilson collapsed, came out and started CPR Mouth to Mouth Resuscitation on Jackie until he began to breath. Not long after Mr. Gunther was shot in his automobile in Las Vegas and his killer has never been found.

DID YOU KNOW?

The manager of the Phelps Lounge, in Detroit, on Oakland Avenue, shared with us that one night when he was closing he heard a knock on the door. It was Jackie who wanted to come in and get a drink. The manager said, "So I called the owner and ask if I could let Jackie in. He said Yes." So, I let him in. He set down and we drank and had a good time after hours. The manager said, "It is a night that I will never forget."

DID YOU KNOW?

In the bar/club scene from the 1962 movie, "Girls! Girls! Girls!" where Elvis is performing the song, "Return to Sender," it is said that Jackie was actually in the audience.

DID YOU KNOW?

There is a voice recording of Elvis talking to the Million Dollar Quartet, in a December 4, 1956 session, about a guy who sang with Billy Ward and His Dominoes, whom he heard sing his hit, "Don't Be Cruel," in Las Vegas, much better than he. Elvis, did and sang it slower in the key of B.

This was the famous recording session when Elvis returned to Sun Studio, and it is said that Johnny Cash, Carl Perkins, and Jerry Lee Lewis were there, and that Elvis was imitating our dad singing, "Don't Be Cruel."

DID YOU KNOW?

"A Woman, a Lover, a Friend," a 1960 single performed by Jackie made it to #1 on the R&B charts, where it stayed at the top spot for one month. It also charted on the Hot 100, peaking at #15.

DID YOU KNOW?

Jackie was nominated for two Grammys: In 1960, he received a nod for "Lonely Teardrops" in the Best Rhythm and Blues Performance category.

In 1967, he was in the running for "(Your Love Keeps Lifting Me) Higher and Higher" in the category Best Rhythm and Blues Solo Vocal Performance, Male.

DID YOU KNOW?

Before he became famous, Jimi Hendrix joined a package tour featuring Jackie Wilson, Sam Cooke, and the Valentinos, which was Bobby Womack and his brother's band, in 1964, just months before Cooke's tragic death at age 33.

DID YOU KNOW?

While Jackie Wilson and jazz vocalist Arthur Prysock were in Little Rock, Arkansas to perform, a melee ensued, and the singers' tires were slashed before they left to go to Dallas.

DID YOU KNOW?

Jackie Wilson could scat. He does so at the end of his song, "When Will Our Day Come."

DID YOU KNOW?

Jackie Wilson and Linda Hopkins recorded the duets, "I Found Love" and "There's Nothing Like Love."

DID YOU KNOW?

Allegedly, Jackie Wilson had white background singers because conductor and arranger Dick Jacobs said that he didn't have time to teach blacks how to read music due to Jackie's career moving so fast.

DID YOU KNOW?

Otis Redding covered "(Your Love Keeps Lifting Me) Higher and Higher" just months before his untimely death at 26.

In 1975, Martha Reeves also recorded a version of the classic, and two years later Rita Coolidge had a rendition retitled "(Your Love Has Lifted Me) Higher and Higher" that went all the way to #2 on the Hot 100.

DID YOU KNOW?

Jackie Wilson tried to work at the Ford Motor Company foundry for two weeks, but he couldn't do it; so he quit.

DID YOU KNOW?

Nat Tarnopol and Jackie Wilson moved to New York City in 1961 for business purposes.

DID YOU KNOW?

In the early 1950s, rhythm and blues were commonly known by the blanket term "race music," which was used to describe African-American music.

DID YOU KNOW?

Why there has been no movie about Jackie Wilson: The rumor reported by Tony Douglas in his book, **Jackie Wilson: The Man, the Music, the Mob,** *alleges that a project blocked by Jackie's second wife* *was scrapped by Berry Gordy because the non-fiction manuscript submitted made her look heroic and trashed Jackie Wilson and Sam Cooke. He was not going to let that happen because songs he co-wrote that brought Jackie to superstar status also helped Mr. Gordy to earn the much-needed funds to found Motown Records. He also respected Jackie as a man.*

DID YOU KNOW?

Per paperwork from the court, Brunswick Records submitted a petition to the probate court for a movie project for Jackie Wilson. The probate judge denied the petition to make a Jackie Wilson film. Further, the judge closed the Jackie Wilson estate.

DID YOU KNOW?

The Contour's auditioned for Berry Gordy and they were told to come back next year. One of the group members said, "Let's go to Jackie's house to tell him what Berry told them." Jackie said, "Wait here." He went upstairs and he called Berry. He was up there for a while, but when he came back he told the contours to go back and audition. They did and they signed with Motown. The rest is history.

DID YOU KNOW?

On May 12, 1975, Moose of Moose & Da Starks opened, Emceed, and was stage manager for the Jackie Wilson Show in Detroit at the Masonic Temple. It was lots of fun and great stories. I did the same show Moose Zonjie in Flint and Inskter.

DID YOU KNOW?

That Jackie Wilson was into politics. He supported Herbert Humphrey and gave speeches in support of him when he ran for president.

DID YOU KNOW?

Jackie knew Cassius Clay and I (Brenda) met Muhammad Ali in the 90's at Cobo Hall in Detroit. He was a great man.

DID YOU KNOW?

The last show Lil Richard did at the Michigan State Fairgrounds my group and I were on that show and, after we performed, Lil Richard called me on stage with him, introduced me as Jackie Wilson's daughter and spoke highly of Jackie.

DID YOU KNOW?

By 1988, three of Jackie's children with Mama Freda were decease. Denise's death was the result of a drug war. The Detroit Free press quoted Highland Park Detective Hubert Yopp as saying, "She was at the wrong place, at the wrong time. The man claimed to be a known drug user had taken off with drugs and money.

The other man who was chasing him caught up with him (at the shop). The dealer fired six shots at him. The shots were fired just as Denise was leaving the store. She was hit once in the back."

The Detroit News reported, "The 28-year-old man, Gary Johnson, was being charged with Jacqueline Denise's murder. Johnson was released on a $50,000 Bond and that July he himself was gunned down as he entered a home." Mama Freda believes it was retaliation because she was Jackie's daughter.

DID YOU KNOW?

That both Jackie Wilson and Sam Cooke were both leaders of gospel singing groups; Jackie Led The Eveready's and Sam Cooke for The Soul Stirrers

Did You Know?

Sammy Davis, Jr. gave Jackie his break at the Copacabana. Jimmy Smith, Jackie's drummer and friends, said Jackie took the mic out of Sammy's hand on stage and sang Sammy's song for him because Jackie and Sammy Davis Jr.'s longtime friend, Frank Sinatra, blackballed Jackie from being booked in any club in the country.

Frank felt that Jackie was disrespectful by grabbing the mic. This was stated in Tony Douglas's book, "Jackie Wilson: The Man, the Music, the Mob."

Did You Know?

"How could this have happened?" Mr. Sims was quoted as saying that had he still been on the road with Jackie, he would still be alive. From the dinner before the show to the show, what happened? Could it have been something related to the court case and indictment of Brunswick Records and the fact that Jackie was supposed to testify against them?

BIBLIOGRAPHY

Videos

910am Superstation -The Lavonia Perryman Show
Jackie Wilson 20/20 ABC Youtube Al Kasha, March 1, 2012
Accessed November 07, 2018,

>   https://www.youtube.com/watch?v=iC6jQhH0YIQ,
>   references from "Jackie Wilson The Man, The Music, The
>   Mob" By Tony Douglas

America Black Journal .org
America Coming Together Written and sung by Erika Johnson
https://youtu.be/EoS4hFIRLg
Watch World Channel 56.4

America Black Journey.org
Jackie 's Wilson Star on the walk of Fame

America Black Journey.org
2018 Father's Day Interview with Brenda Wilson and Billy Davis

City For Youth project
We Need A City video
https://youtu.be/m-rBTFPV82g

America Black Journey.org—
Hollywood Interview with Brenda And Thelma Stubbs Micthell
https://youtu.be/YKIG6al.c2K

Articles:

Google.com Newspaper Clips

Newspaper-N Detroit News 2016/08/16
Jackie Wilson Street renaming to Honor R&B's "Mr. Excitement" -
   Detroit News

uDiscover Music—Where the street has Jackie Wilson

Free Press—News

Highland Park Christens Jackie Wilson Love for Music—Detroit
   Free Press

The Detroit News

Highland Park Honors Jackie Wilson w/ Street Renaming by Susan
   Whitall

The Detroit Free Press

Highland Park Christens
"Jackie Wilson Lane"
For Music Legends Native son
Keith Matheny, Detroit Free Press

Metro Times

Highland Park to Rename Street After Singer
Jackie Wilson—Detroit Metro Times

Newspapers.com

Jackie Wilson Funeral "84 "—Newspapers.com

Pictures

Elevate Dragonfy— Picture of Hollywood Walk of Fame and Brenda
   Wilson